Gaining Strength for Your Journey
Develop What is *Right* for You

To be the chosen, you must come in agreement with the call. You are exempt from every disqualifier.

Mission: To Proclaim Transformation and Truth

Publisher: Transformed Publishing
Website: www.transformedpublishing.com
Email: transformedpublishing@gmail.com

ISBN: 978-1-953241-15-3 Paperback
ISBN: 978-1-953241-16-0 Hardcover
Printed in the U.S.A.

Gaining Strength for your Journey

Diana Robinson

This book is *dedicated* to you...

You are alive,

so you might as well live your best life!

I would have lost heart, unless I had believed
That I would see the goodness of the Lord
In the land of the living.

Psalm 27:13

"Because he has set his love upon Me,
    therefore I will deliver him;
I will set him on high,
    because he has known My name.
He shall call upon Me, and I will answer him;
I *will be* with him in trouble;
I will deliver him and honor him.
With long life I will satisfy him,
And show him My salvation."

Psalm 91:14-16

Table of Contents

1

Foundation

Gaining Strength for Your Journey puts the lives of great biblical men and women on display to give us hope and assurance that perfection does not come from being perfect, it comes from perfecting what one has: gifts, talents, ideas, passions, desires, resources, relationships, positions, etc. Perfection is a noun - a state of being; perfect is an adjective - a description; and perfecting is a verb - an action word. Therefore, we are called to *do* something with what we already have as a prerequisite for elevation!

I am forever grateful for the word of God that gives us snapshots of men and women, like ourselves, on this journey of life; real people who exercised faith, remained committed to authentic vision even when opposition arose, and overcame adversity.

Sometimes they hit the mark right away, but most of the time it was a lifelong journey of God's mercy, grace, and growth. *Mercy* is when we don't receive a deserved negative consequence. *Grace* is when we receive positive consequences that we did not earn.

Who is Joseph?

The Bible dedicates thirteen chapters in the Old Testament to expound on the life of Joseph, not including all we find out about his lineage in additional chapters. The model of Joseph's life is referenced in the New Testament in Acts 7 and Hebrews 11.

Joseph was a man of authority, who operated in the Spirit of God. He engaged in battle at every point of resistance, armed with the weapons of obedience, integrity, and diligence. Joseph manifested the vision for his life that became a refuge for his family and nations, despite affliction and obstacles. He is an authentic demonstration of a life built on the foundational principles of God.

Psalm 27:10 was proven in Joseph's life, "When my father and my mother forsake me, then the Lord will take care of me." *Forsake* means to abandon or turn away from someone who is counting on you.

A person can be physically present, but still viewed as forsaking a loved one. The reality is, it is impossible for a person to be another person's all-in-all. There are areas within us that can only be nurtured and trained by the Holy Spirit. Thank God that He is Omnipresent, Ever Knowing, the Author (Originator), and the Finisher (Perfecter) of our faith (*see* Hebrews 12:2). This gives us freedom to know that where we lack in relational areas, God is faithful to fill the gaps.

The life of Joseph is an awakening testimony to the power activated by obedience to the great commandments declared by Jesus in Matthew 22:37-39, "...'You shall love the LORD your God with all your heart, with all your soul, and with all your mind.' This is *the* first and great commandment. And *the* second is like it: 'You shall love your neighbor as yourself.'"

Joseph sowed seeds of honor to God, and despite hostile circumstances, seeds of forgiveness and love toward his neighbors. As a result, he reaped a tremendous harvest of provision, change of position, and family reunification.

Our Lord and Savior Jesus Christ endured the route of betrayal and crucifixion to resurrection and ascension. Joseph's life outlines these stages of elevation as well. This is validation that elevation does not come by *hoping* or *wishing*. Elevation must be apprehended with full confidence in the Lord and the guaranteed results generated by the continued working of His principles.

Be encouraged with the words of Moses, as he commissioned Joshua for elevation in Deuteronomy 31:8, "And the Lord, He is the One who goes before you. He will be with you, He will not leave you nor forsake you; do not fear nor be dismayed." In Moses' instruction to not fear nor be dismayed, he bears witness to the fact that things arise along the route of elevation to generate fear and dismay; but as we cling to and move with the One who goes before us, nothing will be impossible.

Gain **S**trength   God must be our only source of expectation. Opportunities and provision come through resources; but God is the ultimate *source* of every resource. Making people or resources our source of expectation, results in disappointment. When God is our source, there is appointment.

Psalm 121
I will lift up my eyes to the hills—
From whence comes my help?
My help *comes* from the Lord,
Who made heaven and earth.
He will not allow your foot to be moved;
He who keeps you will not slumber.
Behold, He who keeps Israel
Shall neither slumber nor sleep.
The Lord *is* your keeper;
The Lord *is* your shade at your right hand.
The sun shall not strike you by day,
Nor the moon by night.
The Lord shall preserve you from all evil;
He shall preserve your soul.
The Lord shall preserve your going out and your coming in
From this time forth, and even forevermore.

Write unto the Lord

Write as you reflect on times when you were disappointed by unfulfilled expectations naively placed on people or resources. Include times of triumph, when God was your sole source, resulting in appointment.

Betrayal

Joseph was hated and rejected by his brothers. Jesus was unable to do many mighty works in His own country because of the people's unbelief (*see* Matthew 13:54-58). Likewise, they were both mocked for the robes they wore and stripped of them (*see* Genesis 37:23 and Matthew 27:31). Joseph and Jesus were both sold for a price. Joseph was sold into slavery by his brothers, and Jesus was sold out to the authorities by His disciple Judas (*see* Genesis 37:28 and Matthew 26:15). Betrayal replaced assumed endearment by those in their circle.

Crucifying the Flesh

Joseph crucified his flesh when he was solicited by a seductress, Potiphar's wife, but was condemned to prison anyway. Great distinguished beauty and charm come to mind when imagining a high-ranking ruler's wife. A man ruled by his flesh would have easily taken the open opportunity to lie with the wife of the man whose house he entered as a slave. However, Joseph was more concerned with honoring God than indulging in the pleasures of lying with Potiphar's wife (*see* Genesis 39:7-9).

Jesus crucified His flesh in prayer in the garden of Gethsemane. He prayed with an exceedingly sorrowful soul as quoted in Matthew 26:39, "O My Father, if it is possible, let this cup pass from Me; nevertheless, not as I will, but as You will." It is a common misconception that Jesus *felt like* going to the cross. In Matthew 26:38-44, Jesus petitioned Father God three times to reveal an alternative route. Ultimately, Jesus submitted to His Father's will despite His feelings.

Salvation: The Release from Shame

Jesus made a *choice* to crucify His flesh *before* He was apprehended, foreseeing the greater completed work. This is confirmed in Hebrews 12:2, "...for the joy that was set before Him endured the cross, despising the shame, and has sat down at the right hand of the throne of God."

Jesus found joy in our opportunity to be reconciled with God through Him and the promise of the Holy Spirit to dwell within us.

> For God so loved the world that He gave His only begotten Son, that whoever believes in Him should not perish but have everlasting life. For God did not send His Son into the world to condemn the world, but that the world through Him might be saved.
>
> John 3:16-17

> But this He spoke concerning the Spirit, whom those believing in Him would receive; for the Holy Spirit was not yet given, because Jesus was not yet glorified.
>
> John 7:39

> But the Helper, the Holy Spirit, whom the Father will send in My name, He will teach you all things, and bring to your remembrance all things that I said to you.
>
> John 14:26

Jesus *despised* the shame - He *hated* the shame! Did He have anything to be ashamed about? No, what He hated was the shame that we harbor when we sin. Not God-given shame, but the shame that comes when we condemn ourselves.

The origin of shame is explained in Genesis 3. After Adam and Eve ate of the fruit of the tree of knowledge of good and evil in the Garden of Eden, they were ashamed and immediately sewed fig leaves together to make coverings for themselves. They heard the sound of the Lord God as He walked in the garden and they hid among the trees.

The Lord still sought fellowship with them after they sinned. It was Adam and Eve who put barriers between themselves and God because of their shame. God explained the consequences of sin and mercifully made them tunics of skin and clothed them. Adam and Eve were sent out of the Garden of Eden and a guard was set around the tree of life. If Adam and Eve partook of the tree of life, they would have been sealed in sin, which is never God's desire for anyone.

The first shedding of blood noted in the Bible happened when God made Adam and Eve tunics of skin to *temporarily* cover their sins. The shedding of animal blood became the ceremonial custom throughout the Old Testament and was done continuously until Jesus' blood was shed once and for all, for all sin. "In Him we have redemption through His blood, the forgiveness of sins, according to the riches of His grace" (Ephesians 1:7). His blood also cleanses our conscience from dead works, including shame, to serve the living God.

> Not with the blood of goats and calves, but with His own blood entered the Most Holy Place once for all, having obtained eternal redemption. For if the blood of bulls and goats and the ashes of a heifer, sprinkling the unclean, sanctifies for the purifying of the flesh, how much more shall the blood of Christ, who through the eternal Spirit offered Himself without spot to God, cleanse your conscience from dead works to serve the living God?
>
> Hebrews 9:12-14

Gain Strength   The devil maneuvers, through sin, to layer people with the burdening consuming weight of shame.

Isaiah 59:1-2
Behold, the Lord's hand is not shortened,
That it cannot save;
Nor His ear heavy,
That it cannot hear.
But your iniquities have separated you from your God;
And your sins have hidden *His* face from you,
So that He will not hear.

John 3:17 explicitly tells us, "For God did not send His Son into the world to condemn the world, but that the world through Him might be saved." God loves you. There is nothing you can do to make God love you any more, and there is nothing you can do to make God love you any less. He all inclusively unconditionally loves you.

Write unto the Lord

Identify and reflect on a life decision or unsolicited wicked work that resulted in shame.

Reflect, release, and extend the mercy and grace you have found in Christ to *that* person or circumstance.

Salvation is composed of three parts: justification, sanctification, and glorification. The shed blood of Jesus Christ justifies us. God looks at us just as we never sinned. Justification is fulfilled through confession and belief, as explained in Romans 10:9-10, "that if you confess with your mouth the Lord Jesus and believe in your heart that God has raised Him from the dead, you will be saved. For with the heart one believes unto righteousness, and with the mouth confession is made unto salvation."

Sanctification is our journey with Jesus from justification until the time we depart from this earth. It is the continuous transformation to become more and more Christlike, but it is not measured with a man-made rubric. Along the way, He loves us just the same and is not ashamed to call us brethren. Remember, there is nothing we can do that will make God love us any more, and there is nothing we can do that will make God love us any less. Hebrews 2:11 assures us, "For both He who sanctifies and those who are being sanctified are all of one, for which reason He is not ashamed to call them brethren."

Glorification takes place in the twinkling of an eye, when we are transported from this earth to heaven, as confirmed in 2 Corinthians 5:8, "We are confident, yes, well pleased rather to be absent from the body and to be present with the Lord."

Jesus sat down at the right hand of the throne of God and we are seated with Him as joint heirs. We are given this edification in Romans 8:17, "and if children, then heirs—heirs of God and joint heirs with Christ, if indeed we suffer with Him, that we may also be glorified together."

Resurrection & Ascension

Joseph was committed to the pit, then the prison, and Jesus was committed to the tomb. Joseph's life was resurrected from ruins to ruler over all the land of Egypt. In Genesis 45:8 Joseph told his brothers, "So now *it was* not you *who* sent me here, but God; and He has made me a father to Pharaoh, and lord of all his house, and a ruler throughout all the land of Egypt." With resurrection power comes ascension. By way of Joseph, the posterity of Israel, about seventy family members were grafted into the land of benefit–Goshen.

It was the voice of popular opinion that demanded Jesus be crucified. The people were faced with the choice of releasing unto them a rebellious murderer, Barabbas, or Jesus. The multitude raised up their voices against Jesus and prevailed (*see* Luke 23:13-25). They chose rebellion over Jesus. We also are faced with these two options daily: rebellion or Jesus. Pilate allowed the magnitude of the sound, from the voices of the people, to infect his decision making and to go against what Pilate knew to be right.

Romans 8:28 venerates, "And we know that all things work together for good to those who love God, to those who are the called according to *His* purpose." The crucifixion served great purpose to reconcile us to God for eternity. Moreover, the resurrection and ascension released access to the abundant life here on earth. Jesus resurrected on the third day with an additional set of keys. In addition to the keys of the kingdom of heaven, Jesus holds the keys of hades and death:

> And I [Jesus] will give you the keys of the kingdom of heaven, and whatever you bind on earth will be bound in heaven, and whatever you loose on earth will be loosed in heaven.
>
> Matthew 16:19 (emphasis mine)

> I [Jesus] am He who lives, and was dead, and behold, I am alive forevermore. Amen. And I have the keys of Hades and of Death.
>
> Revelation 1:18 (emphasis mine)

Through Jesus' ascension we have also ascended. Ephesians 2:5-6 states, "even when we were dead in trespasses, [God] made us alive together with Christ (by grace you have been saved), and raised *us* up together, and made *us* sit together in the heavenly *places* in Christ Jesus."

We are joint heirs seated with Christ in heavenly places, grafted into the family of God, in possession of the keys to unlock and exit every dead constricting area of our life. On our key ring, we also have the necessary keys to unlock and enter every good thing the Father has for us in this earth realm, holistically for our body, mind, and spirit.

Gain Strength

You are exempt from every dis-qualifier. God is seeking those who are in position to be used to fulfill His word.

Deuteronomy 9:5
It is not because of your righteousness or the uprightness of your heart *that* you go in to possess their land, but because of the wickedness of these nations *that* the Lord your God drives them out from before you, and that He may fulfill the word which the Lord swore to your fathers, to Abraham, Isaac, and Jacob.

Write unto the Lord

Identify some thoughts that are negatively impacting you because they are in the *womb* instead of the *tomb*. What are some thoughts or ideas that are in the *tomb* but should be in the *womb*? Remember, through Christ (the anointing), you are exempt from every disqualifier.

Genuine vs. Counterfeit

Joseph and Jesus both made landmark statements, which must become part of our thinking and reasoning process as born-again believers:

Joseph declared, "But as for you, you meant evil against me; *but* God meant it for good, in order to bring it about as *it is* this day, to save many people alive."

Genesis 50:20

Jesus declared, "The thief does not come except to steal, and to kill, and to destroy. I [Jesus] have come that they may have life, and that they may have *it* more abundantly."

John 10:10 (emphasis mine)

In order to adequately discern between the genuine and the counterfeit, we must have *hands on* practical experience with the genuine. Knowing the attributes of the genuine, allows us to recognize the counterfeit. If there is no genuine experience, we can easily accept the counterfeit as real.

During the years I worked as a bank teller, my hands touched a lot of money. That hand-to-hand contact with the genuine, allowed me to be able to detect counterfeit bills. The counterfeit bills I personally identified entered the bank through business deposits from fast food restaurants and convenience stores. Because of limited experience with the genuine, the initial receiver released items of value in exchange for a worthless counterfeit bill, and in return experienced loss. We as the banking institute that detected the counterfeit bill, did not experience any loss. We simply subtracted the amount of the counterfeit bill from the total of the deposit. The one who discerns and separates the counterfeit from among the genuine, will suffer no loss.

I experienced another life example demonstrating this principle when my parents had a surplus of snow-on-the-mountain bushes in their yard. I dug some up and planted them at my house. Knowing they reproduce easily and often; I was allowing similar colored weeds that started sprouting up around the base of the bushes to remain in my garden. Still unsure if these were genuine, I asked my dad several times what the seedlings look like. He repeatedly gave me the same response, "They look just like the bush."

At that time, I had no reference point because I had not yet seen a genuine seedling with my eyes, and I reasoned that the counterfeit weeds *might* be the seedlings because they looked so similar. Then one day, I saw a genuine seedling. And guess what it looked like? *Just like the bush*, like my dad said many times. After seeing the genuine, all the counterfeits were removed and never again given access to the garden.

This essential concept must also be applied to relationships. My husband and I married after knowing each other only seventy-seven days. This year, 2021, we celebrated 13 years of marriage. We both had multiple counterfeit relationships in the past. I was even engaged twice before meeting my genuine husband. Although I knew within, I would not follow through to marry neither of those men, I allowed myself to waste time and put myself through unnecessary heart games.

Mutually, my husband and I both knew we were to marry. It is hard to explain when people ask us the question, "How did you know *that* was the one?"

Now I know, it was an unction of the Holy Spirit – spiritual recognition. We just knew. This assurance cannot be articulated with words of human reasoning.

Prior to ever being married, a woman forever impacted my thinking with this wise and true statement, "God has a plan for us as individuals and also as married couples." At the time we met, my husband and I were moving in the same direction, fully desiring to live the purpose and plan of God for our lives and His design for marriage. We were not unevenly yoked and have found perpetual strength for our journey together. As the saying goes, *it is not always easy, but it is worth it*!

Nothing truly prepares a person for marriage. Eliminating the counterfeit, confirming the genuine, honoring the marriage covenant above all – from better to better; from wealth to wealth; from health to health; to love and to cherish, from life to life, and finding grace for your appointed position as husband and wife solidify and secure marriage. 1 Thessalonians 3:3 reminds us, "that no one should be shaken by these afflictions; for you yourselves know that we are appointed to this."

If we honestly cross-reference these concrete examples with our lives, we will remember instances when we gave genuine and valuable time, emotions, and/or things, in exchange for something or someone counterfeit, and as a result suffered loss.

Genesis 50:20 and John 10:10 give us the measure to sort and classify all aspects of life. Hands on practical contact with God builds a genuine relationship with Him. With full assurance, His attributes are revealed *to* us, then *through* us to others. We learn to discern what is genuinely from God and what is counterfeit sent by the enemy to steal, kill, destroy, and distract.

Gain Strength Differentiating between the genuine and counterfeit can be done by using the word of God as the measuring line and final authority for every circumstance.

Use this space to reflect on the thoughts expressed in this section, *Genuine vs. Counterfeit.* **Write unto the Lord**

Develop What is *Right* for You

2

Identity

Marked

Joseph was born from the womb of Rachel, who was previously called barren. Joseph was the eleventh son of Jacob and the first son of Rachel, Jacob's beloved wife.

Joseph experienced the evident love of his father Jacob, but endured the loss of his mother, Rachel, to death as she gave birth to his dear younger brother Benjamin. In Genesis 37 we are introduced to seventeen-year-old Joseph, who lived in a household consisting of his ten older half-brothers, his younger brother Benjamin, and a half sister, along with their mothers. Joseph had favor in the eyes of his father which bred hostility amongst his brothers.

> Now Israel [Jacob] loved Joseph more than all his children; because he *was* the son of his old age. Also he made him a tunic of *many* colors.
>
> Genesis 37:3 (emphasis mine)

Marked for greatness with the colorful robe of his destiny, Joseph became a target for assassination by the enemy. The Bible doesn't explicitly tell us what colors were featured on the robe. For the purpose of this book, as an outline to present the inclusiveness of the message, let's infer:

YELLOW - The color of the sun, the moon, and the eleven stars that bowed.

BLACK - The color of the pit, because he was hated by his brothers.

GREEN - The color of money, because he was sold into slavery.

PURPLE - The color of royalty, because he was promoted by God.

FUCHSIA - The color of the seductress, because he fled sexual immorality.

GRAY - The color of the cell, because he was falsely accused.

WHITE - The color of purity, because he possessed the Spirit of God.

RED - The color of recompense, because he recovered all.

GOLD - The color of splendor, representing the goodness of Goshen.

Gain Strength

Joseph was adorned with an exterior visible mark, in the form of a robe. It demonstrated the love of his father and the hope and significance of his calling. This same robe was later torn from Joseph in bitterness and envy, dipped in the blood of an animal, and presented back to his father by his brothers, as Joseph's demise. Sudden terror consumed Jacob. "And he recognized it and said, '*It is* my son's tunic. A wild beast has devoured him. Without doubt Joseph is torn to pieces'" (Genesis 37:33).

Negative assumptions drawn from exterior circumstances *only*, became the source of Jacob's internal imprisonment.

Even though the exterior robe was removed, the mark and call of God remained.

Psalm 40:7
Then I said, "Behold, I come;
In the scroll of the book *it is* written of me.

Write unto the Lord

Have you found the place where it is written of you? What is the vision you have been specifically designed to manifest during your lifetime?

_____

_____

_____

_____

_____

_____

_____

_____

_____

_____

_____

_____

_____

_____

_____

_____

_____

_____

_____

Jacob's Deception

Growing up, Jacob sowed seeds of deception. Jacob just cooked a stew when his twin brother Esau came in weary from the field. Jacob solicited Esau's birthright in exchange for bread and the lentil stew.

Both men had been operating in their assignment, as introduced in Genesis 25:27, "...Esau was a skillful hunter, a man of the field; but Jacob was a mild man, dwelling in tents." In design, these two equally important assignments complement one another; but deceptive motives resulted in corruption. In his weariness, Esau did not see the value in his birthright (*see* Genesis 25:29-34).

Jacob again sowed seeds of deception when he carried out a conspiracy, orchestrated by his mother Rebekah, to finagle his twin brother Esau's blessing. The father's blessing of the firstborn son was entitled to Esau, but received by Jacob, as a result of Rebekah and Jacob's deceptive tactics (*see* Genesis 27). Rebekah then directed Jacob to arise and flee because Esau intended to kill Jacob. This set Jacob off on a journey and over time, through a series of events, he was formed into Israel.

On his journey, Jacob served in Laban's house for fourteen years in exchange for Laban's daughters Leah and Rachel to become his wives, and six years for his flocks. Within these twenty years, Laban changed Jacob's wages ten times (*see* Genesis 31:7; 41).

Jacob agreed to serve Laban for seven years in order to fulfill his desire to marry Rachel. At the end of the seven years, Laban deceived Jacob and presented him with his older daughter Leah, as wife, in place of Jacob's beloved Rachel. When Laban was confronted by Jacob, regarding this deception, Laban negotiated in Genesis 29:27, "Fulfill her [Leah's] week, and we will give you this one [Rachel] also for the service which you will serve with me still another seven years."

Leah's Longing

"When the Lord saw that Leah was unloved, He opened her womb; but Rachel was barren" (Genesis 29:31). This sparked an intense *Battle of the Wombs* between Leah and Rachel. Leah consecutively bore Jacob four sons and named them according to the most inward cry of her heart:

> Reuben: "...The LORD has surely looked on my affliction. Now therefore, my husband will love me."
>
> Genesis 29:32

> Simeon: "...Because the LORD has heard that I am unloved, He has therefore given me this son also..."
>
> Genesis 29:33

> Levi: "...Now this time my husband will become attached to me, because I have borne him three sons..."
>
> Genesis 29:34

> Judah: "...Now I will praise the LORD..."
>
> Genesis 29:35

Leah strived to earn the love of her husband through childbearing. Year by year, she desired to *earn* a more esteemed position in the sight of her husband as she bore him sons. Each time she named them with an expression of her emotions and desires. The birth of Judah raised the score in the *Battle of the Wombs* to Leah-4 and Rachel-0. An internal eruption of temporary satisfaction took place as Leah declared in Genesis 29:35, "Now I will praise the Lord."

Leah spent most of her life emotionally defeated and competing for fulfillment. She failed to embrace and activate her position of honor, entered into through the marriage covenant. Evidenced in Genesis 49:31, prior to the death of Israel (Jacob), he commanded to be buried in the burying place of his grandparents, Abraham and Sarah; his parents, Isaac and Rebekah; and where he previously buried Leah, who preceded Jacob in death, therefore, honoring Leah's marital covenant position.

Leah spent a lifetime trying to earn a position she already obtained via covenant. How often do we, as Christians, fail to enter our rightful role and endowment as the bride of Christ? How much time do we spend faltering between two opinions? How much energy do we expend seeking to earn righteousness that can never be earned? Can you imagine the frustration of trying to find a route to the place where you already are? Any effort of travel is a waste of time and resources.

As joint heirs with Christ, we are not striving *for* victory; we are operating *from* the place of victory! This is a liberating revelation of empowerment. Jacob's beloved wife Rachel, who he was emotionally bound to, died and was buried on the way to Ephrath; there Jacob set a pillar on her grave (*see* Genesis 35:19-20). Leah, bound by covenant position, later died and was buried in the place of honor among the patriarchs and matriarchs.

Rachel's Desire

> Now when Rachel saw that she bore Jacob no children, Rachel envied her sister, and said to Jacob, "Give me children, or else I die!" And Jacob's anger was aroused against Rachel, and he said, "*Am* I in the place of God, who has withheld from you the fruit of the womb?"
>
> Genesis 30:1-2

Rachel cried out to man (Jacob), but there is no evidence that she yet brought her petition to God. Jacob's anger was kindled, and he reminded Rachel that he was not in the place of God.

With desperation and urgency, Rachel gave her servant Bilhah to Jacob as wife for Bilhah to birth children on Rachel's behalf. Bilhah consecutively bore Jacob two sons, which Rachel named expressing her excitement. This put Rachel on the scoreboard in the *Battle of the Wombs*; Leah-4, and Rachel-2, via Bilhah.

> Dan: "...God has judged my case; and He has also heard my voice and given me a son..."
>
> Genesis 30:6

Naphtali: "...With great wrestlings I have wrestled with my sister, and indeed I have prevailed..."

Genesis 30:8

No longer content, Leah retaliated and gave Jacob her servant Zilpah as wife, when she stopped bearing. Zilpah consecutively bore Jacob two sons, who Leah named:

Gad: "...A troop comes..."

Genesis 30:11

Asher: "...I am happy, for the daughters will call me blessed..."

Genesis 30:13

Leah then conceived again and bore Jacob an additional two sons and one daughter, who Leah named:

Issachar: "...God has given me my wages, because I have given my maid to my husband..."

Genesis 30:18

Zebulun: "...God has endowed me with a good endowment; now my husband will dwell with me, because I have borne him six sons..."

Genesis 30:20

Dinah: "Afterward she bore a daughter, and called her name Dinah."

Genesis 30:21

Then God remembered Rachel. God listened to her and opened her womb (*see* Genesis 30:22). This signifies that her cry changed from a cry to man in Genesis 30:1-2; to a genuine cry to God that He heard and responded to, "And she conceived and bore a son, and said, "God has taken away my reproach" (Genesis 30:23). Rachel named her son Joseph, prophetically declaring she would have a second son.

> Joseph: "...The LORD shall add to me another son."
>
> Genesis 30:24

As they journeyed from Bethel to Ephrath, Rachel went into labor with her second son, who was Jacob's twelfth son, and she died. The final score in the *Battle of the Wombs* was Leah: 8 sons and 1 daughter, including Zilpah's sons; and Rachel: 4 sons, including Bilhah's sons.

> And so it was, as her soul was departing (for she died), that she called his name Ben-Oni; but his father called him Benjamin. So Rachel died and was buried on the way to Ephrath (that is, Bethlehem). And Jacob set a pillar on her grave, which is the pillar of Rachel's grave to this day.
>
> Genesis 35:18-20

Ben-oni: The name chosen by Rachel, literally means son of my sorrow.

Benjamin: The name chosen by Jacob, literally means son of the right hand.

Gain Strength

For many years, Rachel was burdened by the weight she carried throughout her wait to bear children. The whole time she condemned her own barrenness, she beheld the very eggs within herself assigned to come forth as Joseph and Benjamin at the *set time*. She died after she gave birth to Benjamin. Her life, like ours, was on a prophetic clock. I wonder *if* she had consciously known the timeline of her life, ahead of time, *if* she would have more intentionally enjoyed her life and made each day count to a greater degree.

What do you think? Can you relate to *rushing* time without intentionally enjoying the journey? Explain.

Write unto the Lord

The Forming of Israel

In Jacob's life, he was manipulated by his mother to pursue the position of his brother. He was then sent approximately four hundred miles away from his immediate family to Haran. There he was manipulated by Laban to take the older daughter before the younger and had his wages changed ten times while working another man's vision. Jacob came to the realization that he must break free from working under the bondage of other people's visions to pursue what God had for him.

Jacob saw the countenance of Laban was not favorable to him as before, and the Lord instructed Jacob to, "Return to the land of your fathers and to your family, and I will be with you" (Genesis 31:2-3). The word is clearly declared but Jacob carried a burden of fear. Fear of crossing paths with his twin brother Esau, who Jacob wronged in the past. Jacob made plans to divide his family and possessions in case of an attack. He also sent a large present of livestock ahead, in an attempt to appease Esau (*see* Genesis 32:7-8; 13-15; 20).

On the journey, Jacob found himself left alone to wrestle at the altar for his destiny. His father Isaac's prayers were enough to break barrenness off his mother so he could enter the earth (*see* Genesis 25:21). His mother Rebekah's scheme caused him to receive the blessing deemed for the firstborn (*see* Genesis 27:6-10).

Despite the efforts of others, Jacob needed more, which could only come from wrestling at the altar by himself for himself. Jacob and a Man wrestled until the breaking of day.

And He said, "Let Me go, for the day breaks." But he said, "I will not let You go unless You bless me!" So He said to him, "What *is* your name?" He said, "Jacob." And He said, "Your name shall no longer be called Jacob, but Israel; for you have struggled with God and with men, and have prevailed."

Genesis 32:26-28

Altars are contact points where altering takes place. Jacob was given the name Israel at this altar, which he named Peniel. "For I have seen God face to face, and my life is preserved" (Genesis 32:30).

Although the Lord released the name Israel, meaning *prevailing with God and man,* in place of the name Jacob, meaning *trickster or deceiver,* he continued to go by the name Jacob. Psalm 107:2 reads, "Let the redeemed of the LORD say so, whom He has redeemed from the hand of the enemy." Too often the redeemed of the Lord refuse to say so.

Jacob was anxious about crossing paths with Esau because of the way they parted in the past. When Esau found out that his father Isaac declared the blessing of the firstborn over his brother Jacob, Esau put a demand on his father.

And Esau said to his father, "Have you only one blessing, my father? Bless me - me also, O my father!" And Esau lifted up his voice and wept. Then Isaac his father answered and said to him: "Behold, your dwelling shall be the fatness of the earth, and the dew of heaven from above. By your sword you shall live, and you shall serve your brother; and it shall come to pass, when you become restless, that you shall break his yoke from your neck."

Genesis 27:38-40

In this blessing, it is explicitly stated that when Esau becomes restless, he shall break the yoke from his neck. Sometime, during Jacob and Esau's twenty years of separation, Esau made a quality decision to release himself from the entanglement of offense and unforgiveness. He became restless and broke free of the yoke.

On the contrary, people sometimes become restful when bound. Restfulness is evidenced by becoming complacent, or giving way to anger and unforgiveness, which are the roots of bitterness. Restlessness is a desire to be free *coupled* with doing the work to be *made* free from the restricting yoke.

A traditional yoke is a piece of equipment that binds two animals together by the neck. An experienced animal and an inexperienced animal are yoked together for training. Animals are also yoked together to force them to work on one accord. Restfulness keeps one yoked to bondage, *going with the flow*. Restlessness takes strategy and strength to become the dominant force to break free.

There are stories about strong animals being tied to feeble stakes. They have the physical power to break free but remain bound because their past attempts to free themselves when they were younger, smaller, and unequipped failed. Even though they are now grown and well able in stature, they limit themselves in their minds because of previous discouragement and disappointment.

In Genesis 33:10 Jacob tells Esau, "...inasmuch as I have seen your face as though I had seen the face of God, and you were pleased with me." This kind of forgiveness and pleasant peace on the face of Esau can only be attributed to the mercy, grace, healing, and wholeness found in God, our source.

After this encounter, Jacob began to refer to his brother Esau as *my lord*: further confirmation that the yoke was broken from Esau's neck. There is no evidence of any type of communication from the time Jacob fled because Esau intended to kill him (*see* Genesis 27:41) until now. Esau won in the invisible arena: he had victory over his emotions, which produced visible results.

Being restless is to choose obedience to the word of God, signifying confidence in His results and refusal to be conformed to the world. The Bible gives us specific instructions to take off certain attributes, or *garments*, that contaminate and block desired results and gives counsel of the deemed attributes to put on.

> But now you yourselves are to put off all these: anger, wrath, malice, blasphemy, filthy language out of your mouth. Do not lie to one another, since you have put off the old man with his deeds...
>
> Colossians 3:8-9

Therefore, as *the* elect of God, holy and beloved, put on tender mercies, kindness, humility, meekness, longsuffering; bearing with one another, and forgiving one another, if anyone has a complaint against another; even as Christ forgave you, so you also *must do*. But above all these things put on love, which is the bond of perfection. And let the peace of God rule in your hearts, to which also you were called in one body; and be thankful. Let the word of Christ dwell in you richly in all wisdom, teaching and admonishing one another in psalms and hymns and spiritual songs, singing with grace in your hearts to the Lord. And whatever you do in word or deed, *do* all in the name of the Lord Jesus, giving thanks to God the Father through Him.

Colossians 3:12-17

Gain **S**trength Esau's determination and intrinsic motivation to strive for victory in the invisible brought forth visible tangible proof of the victory.

1 John 1:1
That which was from the beginning, which we have heard, which we have seen with our eyes, which we have looked upon, and our hands have handled, concerning the Word of life—

What you are doing when no one is looking determines your level when you come into view. What you are doing when no one is looking also determines your value when you come into view.

Reflect on the progress you have made so far and what is required to go to the next level of your journey.

Write unto the Lord

After Jacob and Esau reunited, Esau returned to Seir. Jacob told Esau he would meet him in Seir, but he did not. Neither did Jacob go to the destination the Angel of God directed him to in a dream before he left Haran in Genesis 31:13, "I *am* the God of Bethel, where you anointed the pillar *and* where you made a vow to Me. Now arise, get out of this land, and return to the land of your family."

Instead, Jacob got comfortable in various places along the way. He built a house and made booths for his livestock in Succoth, and bought a parcel of land in Shechem (*see* Genesis 33:16-19).

Jacob was directed to a specific covenant place, but he chose the convenient place for many more years. God beckoned Jacob again in Genesis 35:1, "Then God said to Jacob, 'Arise, go up to Bethel and dwell there; and make an altar there to God, who appeared to you when you fled from the face of Esau your brother.'"

When Jacob's mother initially pled for him to leave Beersheba, she told him to stay in Haran for *a few days* until Esau's fury turned away and she would send for him when he could come home (*see* Genesis 27:44). A few days multiplied into twenty years and there is no indication that his mother sent for him to come home.

The distance from Beersheba to Haran is about four hundred miles.[1] God called Jacob back to Bethel and to the land of his family (Beersheba). The distance from Haran to the cities that Jacob chose to inhabit instead

---

[1] "Map of Jacob's Journey to Haran and Back." Headwaters Christian Resources. March 23, 2017. Accessed May 11, 2019. https://headwatersresources.org/map-of-jacobs journey-to-haran-and-back/.

(Succoth and Shechem) is about 335 miles. The distance from Succoth to Bethel is about twenty-five miles and Beersheba is about forty additional miles southwest.

These details show that Jacob was on the outskirts of the place of obedience. He made most of the journey but stopped before entering the fullness of everything God had for him. Trouble came upon his family in the city of Shechem (*see* Genesis 34), a place God did not call him to.

Jacob heard God clearly both times in Genesis 31:13 and Genesis 35:1. Jacob knew the exact location of Bethel. Jacob named Bethel and made a vow to God at Bethel when he initially departed from Beersheba to Haran:

> Then Jacob awoke from his sleep and said, "Surely the LORD is in this place, and I did not know *it*." And he was afraid and said, "How awesome *is* this place! This *is* none other than the house of God, and this *is* the gate of heaven!"
>
> Then Jacob rose early in the morning, and took the stone that he had put at his head, set it up as a pillar, and poured oil on top of it. And he called the name of that place Bethel; but the name of that city had been Luz previously. Then Jacob made a vow, saying, "If God will be with me, and keep me in this way that I am going, and give me bread to eat and clothing to put on, so that I come back to my father's house in peace, then the LORD shall be my God.
>
> Genesis 28:16-21

God performed all Jacob petitioned in these verses: He was with him; He kept him; He gave him bread to eat and clothing to put on; and He brought him back in peace. In fact, God gave Jacob more than he ever asked for. Jacob's lineage from his loins were the chosen heads of the tribes of God's people. Jacob was so close to the *covenant* place, so why did he choose the *convenient* place, only twenty-five miles from Bethel? The key is in Genesis 28:22 and 35:2-3.

> And this stone which I have set as a pillar shall be God's house, and of all that You give me I will surely give a tenth to You.
>
> Genesis 28:22

> And Jacob said to his household and to all who *were* with him, "Put away the foreign gods that are among you, purify yourselves, and change your garments. Then let us arise and go up to Bethel; and I will make an altar there to God, who answered me in the day of my distress and has been with me in the way which I have gone."
>
> Genesis 35:2-3

Exiting Beersheba to Haran, Jacob made a vow to consecrate his possessions to God by giving a tenth to Him. Somewhere along the way, Jacob allowed the entertainment of foreign gods among him. Foreign gods turn attention away from the True and Living God, preventing full submission. Jacob knew that God is not a God of mixtures. He is a God of solutions.

In a mixture, each component retains its properties and can be separated. For example, a salad is a mixture. Each part (lettuce, tomato, cucumber, etc.) can be mixed together in a bowl and again separated. A solution is different. The components do not retain their separate properties. For example, Kool-Aid is a solution. Each part (water, sugar, drink mix) are combined and they cannot be easily separated again.

The heart of God is *not* for His children to live a life of mixtures; conveniently separating Him from components of life. His heart is for us to combine with Him as a solution in all aspects and areas of life.

We are called to be the *salt of the earth*. God's word and the Holy Spirit are often referred to as *water* (*see* Matthew 5:13; Ephesians 5:26; John 7:38). Salt combined with water is a solution.

After almost thirty years (about twenty years in Haran and extended time in Succoth and Shechem), Jacob returned to the covenant place of Bethel. God evidenced His long-suffering and faithfulness, as He once again, declared to Jacob the name Israel and reiterated the promise.

> And God said to him, "Your name *is* Jacob; your name shall not be called Jacob anymore, but Israel shall be your name." So He called his name Israel. Also God said to him: "I *am* God Almighty. Be fruitful and multiply; a nation and a company of nations shall proceed from you, and kings shall come from your body.
>
> Genesis 35:10-11

As they journeyed from Bethel on their way to Bethlehem, this is the moment in time Rachel died giving birth to Benjamin. Israel stopped short again, just ten miles away from where his family was in Hebron, and dwelt beyond the tower of Eder where another dysfunction transpired in the family. Reuben, Israel's first-born son, laid with Bilhah (*see* Genesis 35:19-22).

Israel and his family then traveled the remaining distance to reunite with his father Isaac who was in Hebron (*see* Genesis 35:27). *Look at God!* In Genesis 27:2 Isaac said, "Behold now, I am old. I do not know the day of my death." Favorably, Isaac lived many more years, as evidenced by Jacob returning to him after more than thirty years of separation, and them dwelling together again until Isaac's death at 180 years old. Isaac, "old and full of days," was buried by both his sons, Esau and Jacob (*see* Genesis 35:28-29). Mercy and Grace refused to let Isaac die without being reconciled with his sons.

Gain Strength Often our greatest agitation is an indication of what we were sent to the earth to solve. The continued agitation is designed to break forth the solution inside of you.

2 Corinthians 4:7
But we have this treasure in earthen vessels, that the excellence of the power may be of God and not of us.

John 1:16, AMP
For out of His fullness [the superabundance of His grace
and truth] we have all received grace upon grace
[spiritual blessing upon spiritual blessing, favor upon
favor, and gift heaped upon gift].

As you meditate on different areas of your life, ask yourself, "Am I operating in the convenient place or the covenant place? Am I merely **W**rite unto the **Lord** *mixed* with purpose externally, or has the *hidden treasure* in my earthen vessel been activated as a solution to an issue of humanity?

Dysfunctional Cycles

Cycles are repetitive actions. Repeated circular movement causes dizziness, blurry vision, and nausea. Think about it! Constant spinning changes the perception of reality. An onset of symptoms mimicking illness develop, such as confusion, instability, deteriorating vision, and even vomiting.

The enemy's desire is for us to be *caught up* in cycles vainly exerting energy to move aimlessly between sudden highs and sudden lows but never advancing. Some results include physical, mental, and spiritual exhaustion; fear; and an inability to see clearly.

Relief from being jerked around and around only comes when we break out of the cycle! One cut in the circle breaks the momentum. Cut and pull to change the form from circular to an extended ray of elevation.

Yes, it is easier said than done, but you are well able. The ability *to do* comes from revelation of truth found in God's word and obedience to it. Paul directs us to shift our position in spiritual battles from defense to offense "...being ready to punish all disobedience when your obedience is fulfilled" (2 Corinthians 10:6).

For me personally, my breakout scripture was Romans 6:21, "What fruit did you have then in the things of which you are now ashamed? For the end of those things is death." There is an expression, *hindsight is 20/20*, meaning, if I would have seen clearly then, what I see now, I never would have tolerated *that*.

The Holy Spirit revealed to me a multi-generational cycle of abandonment among the patriarchs. Isaac endured over three decades of separation between himself and Jacob. Jacob later experienced more than two decades of separation from his own son Joseph.

Don't forget, Jacob's mother, Rebekah, told Jacob to stay in Haran for a *few days* until Esau's fury turned away. Rebekah did not disclose to Isaac that she wanted Jacob away from home because Esau intended to kill Jacob. Rebekah told Isaac she did not want Jacob to take a *daughter of the land* they dwelt in as a wife. Under false pretenses, Isaac charged Jacob to go to Haran to the daughters of Laban to find a wife (*see* Genesis 27:46 – Genesis 28:2).

So much time passed and there is no indication in the scriptures that either Rebekah or Isaac sought Jacob's return. When Jacob's own son Joseph became separated from him, also under false pretenses, neither did Jacob inquire further nor seek Joseph's return.

Although abandoned himself, Joseph proved able to break this generational cycle. Joseph kept his sons close and enjoyed them to the third generation.

Commit to Change

Therefore, if anyone is in Christ, *he* is a new creation; old things have passed away; behold, all things have become new.

2 Corinthians 5:17

Old things have passed away is not just passing a point in time; it means that old things (actions, thoughts, beliefs) before Christ are dead. When we bury the dead, we do not dig them up again. On resurrection morning, Jesus' loved ones came to the tomb and were asked, "Why do you seek the living among the dead? He is not here, but is risen!" (*see* Luke 24:5-6). This is a great question to ponder during times of self-reflection. Roaming around tombs brings gloom.

The same resurrection power that raised Jesus Christ from the dead dwells in us and is available to catapult us from the tomb. "But if the Spirit of Him who raised Jesus from the dead dwells in you, He who raised Christ from the dead will also give life to your mortal bodies through His Spirit who dwells in you" (Romans 8:11).

Revival is to come alive again; back to the original design. When Jesus was crucified, His skin was ripped and shredded. On the third day, Jesus began appearing to His loved ones and His skin was intact. The prints of the nails were visible, but the wounds were not open. Jesus continued to appear over the course of forty days to strengthen and teach believers before He ascended. He was not immediately recognized because the last Jesus they saw appeared defeated and torn up (*see* Acts 1:3 and John 20:27). They did not expect such a display of transformation stemming from the resurrection power.

We must set our expectations higher. Jesus is our example. Commit to be transformed to the point that you don't look like what you have been through, and glorify God.

Revelation 12:11 gives strategic insight to overcome the devil: "And they overcame him by the blood of the Lamb and by the word of their testimony, and they did not love their lives to the death." The first two components - the blood of Jesus and the word of their testimony – are the commonly quoted parts of this verse. However, the third part, *and they did not love their lives to the death*, is essential too.

To be in love with the struggle, tradition, complacency, shame, unforgiveness, fear, etc. halts the newness of *all things* found in Christ Jesus. Look past adverse circumstances, feelings, and opinions unto the *perfect law of liberty*. Obedience to God's perfect law brings freedom and His *perfect love casts out fear*. Fear is not of God; it is a deterrent of the enemy.

> But he who looks into the perfect law of liberty and continues in it, and is not a forgetful hearer but a doer of the work, this one will be blessed in what he does.
>
> James 1:25

> There is no fear in love; but perfect love casts out fear, because fear involves torment. But he who fears has not been made perfect in love.
>
> 1 John 4:18

> For God has not given us a spirit of fear, but of power and of love and of a sound mind.
>
> 2 Timothy 1:7

Change and commitment abide in one another. For change to take place, there must be commitment. As commitments are entered into and followed through with consistency, change must come. The productivity, or *harvest*, of a person's life is dependent upon their commitments. Guiding principles, taught by Pastor Errol Beckford, that have helped me tremendously are, "The things we tolerate will never change. And change is not change until you change!"

Jacob's formation into Israel was a process. Jacob was hesitant to depart from the old and embark on the new. He was urged to look forward but still peeked behind. Physically it is impossible for our eyes to look forward and behind at the same time. Even when using a rearview mirror, it is not possible without shifting or deviating focus.

Awareness that God created, formed, redeemed, named, and claimed us is a source of strength to remain committed to change. "But now, thus says the Lord, who created you, O Jacob, And He who formed you, O Israel: 'Fear not, for I have redeemed you; I have called you by your name; You *are* Mine'" (Isaiah 43:1).

Jesus Christ came into the world and gave His life as a ransom for many. Amnesty has been granted from the stronghold of sin (*see* Matthew 20:28). Nonetheless, people remain bound to the *destiny hijacker* – satan – and his legion of demonic oppression. Why the *none-the-less* portion? How is contentment and security found amid the dangers of the destiny hijacker? What hinders freedom, even after the ransom has been paid?

The Bible is clear, the mercy needed to break the cycle of iniquity is activated by loving God and keeping His commandments (*see* Exodus 20:5-6). The two greatest commandments, expressed by Jesus in Matthew 22:36-40, are to love the Lord your God with all your heart, with all your soul, and with all your mind; and to love your neighbor as yourself. Jesus then challenged us in John 13:34 with a new commandment, "As I have loved you, that you also love one another."

Human tendency is to share what we have an abundance of and withhold what is scarce. Experiencing the love of God for oneself is vital. Submission to God puts us in alignment with God to be filled with the outpouring of His love. We must believe that God is love and He loves us with unconditional agape love! When full and running over with the love of God, we can effectively love our neighbors, aiming to love as He has loved us.

The Holy Spirit gave me an image of a glass, filled with brightly colored liquid, being poured into continuously from a large crystal pitcher containing clear living water. As long as the glass remains in alignment with the flow coming from the pitcher, all the brightly colored liquid is forced out, and the glass runs over with the same clear living water.

The brightly colored liquid represents our sin, shame, polluted mind, and damaged emotions. The clear living water represents the Love of God, His word, and the power of the Holy Spirit. Remain obedient to the position of submission to overcome obstacles.

Submission to God fortifies us and brings change as confirmed in James 4:7, "Therefore submit to God. Resist the devil and he will flee from you." To resist the devil is to resist the temptation to come out from the place of submission. Moses said to the people when Pharaoh's army was pursuing them, and the Red Sea was before them in Exodus 14:13-14, "Do not be afraid. Stand still, and see the salvation of the Lord, which He will accomplish for you today. For the Egyptians whom you see today, you shall see again no more forever. The Lord will fight for you, and you shall hold your peace."

Value the Valuable

People take great precautions not to devalue the things they perceive as valuable. For example, expensive, brand new, freshly painted cars are not driven in the same manner as older cars with a lot of wear and tear. Caution is taken with the valuable car to not drive it in a way or park it in a place where it could be devalued. People who know their great value will not conduct themselves or put themselves into depleting situations.

Likewise, people walk differently in brand new shoes. They alter their walk and watch their steps because of the value placed on the shoes. *Play shoes* or *yard shoes* are worn in the rain or behind a lawn mower; but not so with new shoes. When wearing shoes considered valuable, people are careful not to walk in a manner or an area that would mess them up. Walk with discernment beloved child of God. You are valuable and carry the attributes of your heavenly Father!

God spotlights His children to demonstrate His power and goodness to draw others to Himself. This illumination is affirmed in 2 Corinthians 5:20, "Now then, we are ambassadors for Christ, as though God were pleading through us: we implore *you* on Christ's behalf, be reconciled to God." An ambassador is a high-ranking person who represents his or her own government while living in another country. We are high-ranking representatives of Jesus Christ in this earth realm. God is pleading – desiring to draw the souls of others through the witness of our lives. We must be reconciled to God in order to carry out this imperative charge.

Romans 2:4
Or do you despise the riches of His goodness, forbearance, and longsuffering, not knowing that the goodness of God leads you to repentance?

Gain Strength

After a great victory on Mt. Carmel, Elijah secluded himself in a cave – a cold dark place of limitation and isolation. The still small voice of God drew Elijah out and he wrapped his face in his mantle again which reignited the purpose of his journey (*see* 1 Kings 19:13). The mantle represents the vision; the mark to fulfill the assignment.

Wrap YOUR face in YOUR Mantle, AGAIN!

Don't Give Up On Your Dream...

- Keep the vision closely before your face
- Come out, come out wherever you are
- There is a succession line of kings (earthly leadership) & prophets (spiritual authority) who are waiting on your activation
- You are never alone; there are *yet* a multitude reserved, *Divine Destiny Helpers*

"Yet I have reserved seven thousand in Israel, all whose knees have not bowed to Baal, and every mouth that has not kissed him."
1 Kings 19:18

Write unto the **Lord** Identify dysfunctional cycles in your life. Create and commit to a plan that will bring forth lasting change. God's endless love *is* strength for your journey. Remember, Romans 5:8, "But God demonstrates His own love toward us, in that while we were still sinners, Christ died for us."

3

Dream

Former Days

Joseph was motherless after Rachel's death and Jacob was absent of the woman he fell magnetically in love with. Joseph's birth was announced in Genesis 30. In Genesis 37 Joseph is more articulately introduced.

> Now Jacob dwelt in the land where his father was a stranger, in the land of Canaan. This is the history of Jacob. Joseph, *being* seventeen years old, was feeding the flock with his brothers. And the lad *was* with the sons of Bilhah and the sons of Zilpah, his father's wives; and Joseph brought a bad report of them to his father. Now Israel loved Joseph more than all his children, because he was the son of his old age. Also he made him a tunic of *many* colors. But when his brothers saw that their father loved him more than all his brothers, they hated him and could not speak peaceably to him. Now Joseph had a dream, and he told *it* to his brothers; and they hated him even more. So he said to them, "Please hear this dream which I have dreamed: There we were, binding sheaves in the field. Then behold,

my sheaf arose and also stood upright; and indeed your sheaves stood all around and bowed down to my sheaf." And his brothers said to him, "Shall you indeed reign over us? Or shall you indeed have dominion over us?" So they hated him even more for his dreams and for his words.

Genesis 37:1-8

Imparted in Joseph, at the age of seventeen through a dream, is a glimpse of his destiny. This tremendous vision announced the magnitude of his assignment. Likened to Paul's statement in 1 Corinthians 16:9: "For a great and effective door has opened to me, and *there are* many adversaries." Joseph's adversaries, at this time, came from within his own family – his brothers. Later we will see, as Joseph remained obedient to the vision and continued to do all things wholeheartedly as unto the Lord, their evil intentions were rendered powerless. Little did his brothers know, Joseph was being sent before them to do the works of the Lord in Egypt; which later would become their very own asylum.

Glimpse of the Latter Days

Joseph's latter days in Egypt far exceeded his former days in Canaan. Glorious was the robe of many colors, but it was only a temporary exterior cover, which was ripped off Joseph by his brothers, dipped in animal blood, and deceptively presented to Jacob as Joseph's demise. The robe was a prophetic voice declaring things to come. There is strength to be gained from the word of God, conveying the benefit of travailing perseverance.

"The glory of this latter temple shall be greater than the former," says the LORD of hosts. "And in this place I will give peace," says the LORD of hosts.

Haggai 2:9

Though your beginning was small, Yet your latter end would increase abundantly.

Job 8:7

For the vision is yet for an appointed time; but at the end it will speak, and it will not lie. Though it tarries, wait for it; because it will surely come, it will not tarry.

Habakkuk 2:3

Joseph reaped the latter harvest from the age of thirty years old until his death at 110 years old. When the "vision tarries, wait for it: because it will surely come, it will not tarry," can be equated to pregnancy. Necessary time is needed for a baby to develop in the womb. The discomforts of pregnancy and the pain of labor and delivery are small things, in comparison, to the life-long love and enjoyment of the completed work.

Prophetic Dreams

Joseph's dreams of elevation intimidated his brothers and caused them to hate Joseph even more. His brothers did not see strength in humility, meekness, or honor. They perceived Joseph's prophetic position as superior to theirs, unaware that they were assigned to be heads over nations themselves (*see* Genesis 35:11). Joseph saw his future first and began to cultivate it. Coveting others' gifts distracts and delays oneself from cultivating their own gifts.

Instead of pondering the prophetic dream in his heart only, Joseph spoke it among those who did not have the capacity to support it, as evidenced by their belittlement of Joseph. Meanwhile, God validated His word over the word of Joseph's brothers by giving Joseph a second dream, which was then rebuked by his father.

> Then he dreamed still another dream and told it to his brothers, and said, "Look, I have dreamed another dream. And this time, the sun, the moon, and the eleven stars bowed down to me."
>
> So he told *it* to his father and his brothers; and his father rebuked him and said to him, "What *is* this dream that you have dreamed? Shall your mother and I and your brothers indeed come to bow down to the earth before you?" And his brothers envied him, but his father kept the matter *in mind*.
>
> Genesis 37:9-11

Gain Strength

Joseph's first dream illustrates dominion over the earth (sheaves – terrestrial). Joseph's second dream depicts authority regarding the heavens (solar system – celestial).

People have some control and influence over terrestrial happenings, but the vast elements of the celestial are considered uncontrollable by human influence. Through increased technology, we have observed a small portion of the solar system, but in no way have a proven ability to influence, or have control over elements, past the earth's atmosphere.

As we follow Joseph's journey, we will see that he rose to a place of dominion in society and through the ranks of prestigious positions. He was given divine instruction from God to take control of the controllable, to sustain all of Egypt and the surrounding nations, during an uncontrollable time of famine.

Throughout Joseph's life the word was tested. The ultimate test for us is to remain in faith when things *appear* to be contrary to hope.

Psalm 105:19
Until the time that his word came to pass,
The word of the Lord tested him.

Write unto the Lord

The word and vision for your life will be tested. We must be sustained with His strength for the journey. Strategize your responses during times of testing.

Viability of the Vision

Vision is from God for us. Manifestation is through us for God. Before we were formed in our mother's womb, all our days were already written. The vision was first. Then the person was hand-crafted and named to fulfill the vision by the Creator. Our inward parts were fashioned and molded with all things required to manifest the vision. People were not created and then vision assigned or passed out. Confirmation of this is found in Psalm 139:16, "Your eyes saw my substance, being yet unformed. And in Your book they all were written, The days fashioned for me, When as yet there were none of them."

Significance of the Seed

Over time, both of Joseph's prophetic dreams came to pass. The dreams were seeds beholding vision and purpose. Store displays present seed packets with eye-capturing, brilliantly colored, detailed pictures of desired plants. The reality is, what is in the packet does not visibly match what is on the outside *yet*.

To the pessimist, it is disappointing because the expectation is not immediately met. Because there is no instant gratification, they may give up too soon, seeing little or no value in the seed. To the optimist, it is the beginning of a journey delivering the substance of the previewed picture over time, with the ability to then reproduce after its own kind. This is the God-given purpose for every seed, as emphasized in Genesis 1:12, "And the earth brought forth grass, the herb that yields seed according to its kind, and the tree that yields fruit, whose seed is in itself according to its kind. And God saw that it was good."

Desires of the heart and petitions of the lips are usually released in seed form. When gardening, for best results follow the directions printed on the seed packet. In the same way, the Bible is the guide to achieve optimal results from the seed, which is the word of God (*see* Luke 8:11).

Seeds left in the packet will not germinate: no matter how long they have been there, how much money was paid for them, or how strong the desire is for results. For manifestation, seeds must be planted. Over time, cultivated seeds will produce a harvest, henceforth, *seed-time-harvest* (*see* Genesis 8:22).

Joseph's dreams were seeds received in faith. The biblical definition of faith in Hebrews 11:1 is, "Now faith is the substance of things hoped for, the evidence of things not seen." The *hoped for* is the vision of the completed work, which is the image on the cover of the seed packet. The *evidence of things not seen* is the seed inside the packet. The fact that there is seed in the packet, verifies that there is a mature plant somewhere that brought forth the seed.

Operate in the Way

GPS navigation systems are used to find directions when traveling. Two key pieces of information are required: current location and destination. The GPS can track the current location, but the address of the destination must be entered. Being present at the current location is proof that it exists. Proof of our destination is the fact that it has an address. The possible routes are configured and presented. The operator must select and set which route to take.

In the same way, the Holy Spirit acts as our navigation system. Honestly allow the Holy Spirit to *track* your current location. Write out the destination, which is the vision, in order to receive the route. "All *this*," *said David*, "the LORD made me understand in writing, by *His* hand upon me, all the works of these plans" (1 Chronicles 28:19).

Hold fast to the route. In Psalm 119:109-110 David asserts, "My life is continually in my hand, yet I do not forget Your law. The wicked have laid a snare for me, yet I have not strayed from Your precepts." As the operator, there are many choices we must make along the route. Romans 11:29 tells us, "For the gifts and the calling of God *are* irrevocable." This means that God doesn't take away or change the vision He created us for, or hand it off to someone else. What is for us, *is for us!* Despite where the consequences of our choices take us - the gifts and the calling of God go within us. We can't shake God! He is not following us; He is in us!

Joseph knew where he was. Joseph knew where he was ultimately going. The Lord gave him a glimpse of his destination through his dreams that carried him through a route of adversity. Joseph's mode of travel on the route from seed form, *dreams*; to manifestation, *governor of Egypt*, was obedience. Joseph had an elite destination with only one hard pressed route available. His relentless obedience to the Lord enabled him to overcome every obstacle.

Gain Strength

God's laws, statutes, and commands are general to all. However, His *precepts* are unique and individualized for each of us.

<u>Precepts</u> – the preconceived purpose for your conception; preordained steps as you journey to fulfill your destiny.

The route may not always be easy, but it prepares us to overtake *greater and mightier nations than ourselves.*

Deuteronomy 9:1
"Hear, O Israel: You *are* to cross over the Jordan today, and go in to dispossess nations greater and mightier than yourself, cities great and fortified up to heaven[."]

Judges 3:1-5
Now these *are* the nations which the Lord left, that He might test Israel by them, *that is,* all who had not known any of the wars in Canaan (*this was* only so that the generations of the children of Israel might be taught to know war, at least those who had not formerly known it), ...And they were *left, that He might* test Israel by them, to know whether they would obey the commandments of the Lord, which He had commanded their fathers by the hand of Moses.

Psalm 119:67
Before I was afflicted I went astray, But now I keep Your word.

My pastor, Errol Beckford, taught a message in February 2020 on *time & chance* that gave my husband and I, along with others who received the message, an ariel view to navigate through 2020 and into 2021 during a world-wide pandemic; COVID-19.

My husband's photography and videography business, MR-AH Photography, grew at a rate passing all previous business performance since it began in 2016.

I was inspired to establish Transformed Publishing, with the mandate *to proclaim transformation and truth.* In less than one year, Transformed Publishing launched 7 authors, published 11 books, and established a monthly community newsletter. Many of the new authors told me they started working on their books decades ago but were unsure how to bring them to completion.

Seize opportunities in the midst of chaos, challenges, and calls.

Ecclesiastes 9:11
I returned and saw under the sun that—
The race *is* not to the swift,
Nor the battle to the strong,
Nor bread to the wise,
Nor riches to men of understanding,
Nor favor to men of skill;
But time and chance happen to them all.

Write unto the Lord

As directed in Habakkuk 2:2, "…"Write the vision and make *it* plain on tablets, That he may run who reads it." Write your vision here so you can run with it (not from it).

4

Direction

Divine Direction

Joseph's older brothers were out pasturing the flocks while Joseph remained at home. Joseph was sent out by Israel to check on the well-being of his brothers. Israel was unaware that this would be the last time he saw his son for over two decades. Israel sent Joseph out as a seventeen-year-old boy and later reunited with Joseph as a man in his late thirties, who was governor over all the land of Egypt.

> Then his brothers went to feed their father's flock in Shechem. And Israel said to Joseph, "Are not your brothers feeding the *flock* in Shechem? Come, I will send you to them." So he said to him, "Here I am." Then he said to him, "Please go and see if it is well with your brothers and well with the flocks, and bring back word to me." So he sent him out of the Valley of Hebron, and he went to Shechem. Now a certain man found him, and there he was, wandering in the field. And the man asked him, saying, "What are you seeking?" So he said, "I am seeking my brothers. Please tell me where they are

feeding *their flocks*." And the man said, "They have departed from here, for I heard them say, 'Let us go to Dothan.'" So Joseph went after his brothers and found them in Dothan.

Genesis 37:12-17

While seeking his brothers, Joseph became noticeably lost *wandering* in the field. Joseph was found by a certain man who asked him, "What are you seeking?" It was apparent that Joseph didn't have a purpose in the field; he was out of place. The man did not ask, *who* are you seeking; but *what*. Meaning: *what* could you possibly be looking for here? You are out of place. The certain man *found* Joseph signifying Joseph was *lost*; off course. Without a formal introduction, this director of destiny rerouted Joseph to Dothan.

Dothan is about fifteen miles from Shechem. Joseph was traveling on foot and alone. A moderate-paced walk could have taken between three to five hours depending on the terrain. Joseph did not have modern technology to find his brothers once he arrived in Dothan. There were no cell phones nor messaging technology. Joseph could have reasonably returned home, rationalizing that his brothers were too far away or too hard to find, but Joseph was obedient. He chose to pursue and carry out his father's request despite the circumstances.

Now when they saw him afar off, even before he came near them, they conspired against him to kill him. Then they said to one another, "Look, this dreamer is coming! Come therefore, let us now kill him and cast him into some pit; and we shall say, 'Some wild beast has devoured him.' We shall see what will become of his dreams!" But Reuben heard *it*, and he delivered him out of their hands, and said, "Let us not kill him." And Reuben said to them, "Shed no blood, *but* cast him into this pit which *is* in the wilderness, and do not lay a hand on him"—that he might deliver him out of their hands, and bring him back to his father. So it came to pass, when Joseph had come to his brothers, that they stripped Joseph *of* his tunic, the tunic of *many* colors that *was* on him. Then they took him and cast him into a pit. And the pit was empty; *there was* no water in it.

Genesis 37:18-24

A Seed Committed to the Ground

When Joseph came into his brothers' view, he was mocked for his God-given mark; *this dreamer is coming*. They conspired to negate Joseph's destiny. Their mission was three-fold: kill his dreams, steal his destiny, and destroy his reputation and influence.

Reuben, son of Leah and Joseph's eldest brother, interceded on Joseph's behalf. Reuben suggested they cast Joseph into the pit instead of killing him. Reuben's intention was to later gather Joseph from the pit and bring him back to his father.

Reuben was unwilling to allow the worst thing to happen to Joseph, but he was also unwilling to do the *right* thing. The *right* thing would have been to void the entire evil plot and immediately return Joseph to his father.

Reuben is a mirror of many of us when we decline to engage in the *worst thing*, but we don't choose to do the *right thing;* instead we linger somewhere in the middle with a *good* intention that we will do better next time.

**ain**

trength

More often than we realize, the *good* thing may be deterring us from the *right* thing. Practically speaking, in our day-to-day lives, we can be so consumed doing *good* things that we neglect doing what is *right* for us.

❖ *Right* for our self-care
❖ *Right* for the progression of our goals & purpose
❖ *Right* to advance on our journey
❖ *Rightly* developing our relationship with God, who is the ultimate guide. Psalm 32:8 states, "I will instruct you and teach you in the way you should go; I will guide you with My eye." For the Lord to guide us with His eye, we must develop a close intimate relationship focused on Him in order for us to benefit from His cues.
❖ *Rightly* taking the given opportunities to cherish moments with our loved ones, instead of being too busy with *good* tasks: *Martha, Martha!* (*see* Luke 10:41).

Write unto the **Lord**

Take a moment to reflect on some *good* things that are keeping you from what is *right* for you.

Proverbs 23:4
Do not overwork to be rich;
Because of your own understanding, cease!

We cannot operate by our own understanding alone, we need to know what is *right* for us, according to God's customized precepts for us as individuals, families, communities, churches, and businesses.

Stripped

    When Joseph came to his brothers, they stripped Joseph of the robe of many colors and cast Joseph into a dry pit. This concoction of evil devices later worked together for the good of all Egypt, surrounding nations, and even his brothers themselves. Joseph loved the Lord and continued to work toward manifesting the vision for His purpose. The pit became the ground which the seed of Joseph's life was planted.

> And we know that all things work together for good to those who love God, to those who are the called according to *His* purpose.
>
> Romans 8:28

> "No weapon formed against you shall prosper, and every tongue *which* rises against you in judgment you shall condemn. This *is* the heritage of the servants of the LORD, and their righteousness *is* from Me," says the LORD.
>
> Isaiah 54:17

    In Genesis 37:20, Joseph's brothers made the statement, "We shall see what will become of his dreams!" Unbeknownst to them, despite their efforts, Joseph prospered and all his dreams came to pass exceedingly, abundantly greater than the imagination could fathom.

> God *is* not a man, that He should lie, Nor a son of man, that He should repent. Has He said, and will He not do? Or has He spoken, and will He not make

it good? Behold, I have received a *command* to bless; He has blessed, and I cannot reverse it.

Numbers 23:19-20

Jesus was asked by the governor, Pilate, if He was the *King of the Jews*. Jesus replied, "It is as you say" (*see* Matthew 27:11). Jesus was later adorned in a scarlet robe as a form of mockery.

And they stripped Him and put a scarlet robe on Him. When they had twisted a crown of thorns, they put *it* on His head, and a reed in His right hand. And they bowed the knee before Him and mocked Him, saying, "Hail, King of the Jews!" Then they spat on Him, and took the reed and struck Him on the head. And when they had mocked Him, they took the robe off Him, put His *own* clothes on Him, and led Him away to be crucified.

Matthew 27:28-31

The realization came to pass for the mockers that Jesus was who He said He was after He took His last breath. All creation bore witness: from noon to 3:00 p.m. there was darkness over all the land; the veil of the temple was torn in two from top to bottom; the earth quaked, the rocks were split, and the graves were opened; many bodies of the saints who had fallen asleep were raised; and coming out of the graves after His resurrection, they went into the holy city and appeared to many. The witnesses proclaimed, "Truly this was the Son of God!" (*see* Matthew 27:45-54).

The robes of Joseph and Jesus can be likened to a seed packet. The seed packet, beholding the image of the full manifestation of things to come, must be stripped back, in order to reveal the seed. The seed packet is not alive. Life is only found in the seed within the packet. The seed packet could be embellished in the finest artwork, outlined in pure gold, and adorned with precious jewels, but it will never produce life.

The outer covering is not the source of life. The cliché, "clothes make the man" is not true. The outer man does not make the inner man. The inner man develops the outer man. With or without the elaborate robe, Joseph and Jesus held fast to the integrity and commitment of their inner man ultimately remaining obedient to God.

Light Births Life

The expression, "look at the bright side," can be equated to, "look to the *light*." Creation bears witness to the fact that light causes darkness to flee. The brightness of the light determines its territory. Darkness looms at light's circumference, but for darkness to acquire territory the light must dwindle or be absent. Darkness cannot invade when light shines at its maximum potential.

The illuminating light of the glory of the Lord rises upon us! This is not a light that we are pressured to create nor earn. We receive the light of the glory of the Lord through submission. This principle is validated through-out the Bible. Some scriptures for reference are:

Arise, shine; For your light has come! And the glory of the Lord is risen upon you. For behold, the darkness shall cover the earth, And deep darkness the people; But the Lord will arise over you, And His glory will be seen upon you.

Isaiah 60:1-2

Do not rejoice over me, my enemy; When I fall, I will arise; When I sit in darkness, The LORD will be a light to me.

Micah 7:8

Let your light so shine before men, that they may see your good works and glorify your Father in heaven.

Matthew 5:16

And the light shines in the darkness, and the darkness did not comprehend it.

John 1:5

Then Jesus spoke to them again, saying, "I am the light of the world. He who follows Me shall not walk in darkness, but have the light of life."

John 8:12

I have come as a light into the world, that whoever believes in Me should not abide in darkness.

John 12:46

The Barren Shall Break Forth

The pit Joseph was cast into was empty with no water in it, representing barrenness. Joseph's mother Rachel was one of the six monumental women in the Bible who were called barren. Each child who first broke forth from the womb of each of these women was inevitably influential. This will be elaborated more in Chapter 8 of this book:

- ❖ Sarah (Abraham) begot Isaac
- ❖ Rebekah (Isaac) begot Esau & Jacob
- ❖ Rachel (Jacob) begot Joseph
- ❖ Unnamed woman (Manoah) begot Samson
- ❖ Hannah (Elkanah) begot Samuel
- ❖ Elizabeth (Zacharias) begot John the Baptist

Repeatedly our True and Living God is identified in scripture as *The God of Abraham, Isaac, and Jacob.* Notice the generational lineage: Abraham's son Isaac came from a barren womb. Isaac's son Jacob came from a barren womb. Jacob's son Joseph came from a barren womb. The enemy used barrenness - emptiness and desolation - as an attempt to discourage and discredit the people of God. Travailing faith and God's timing prevailed. Each womb was opened at the set time.

As we watch Joseph's life unfold, we see that through Joseph the cycle of barrenness was broken. Joseph produced children with no struggle. Joseph was recorded as having one wife and no concubines, contrasting his father Jacob and great-grandfather Abraham, who both had children by multiple women.

Gain Strength

Our declarations must be God's ideas for us. Declarations grasp the blueprint from heaven and the granted authorization to move forward, therefore establishing *it* for us. The light gives direction as to how to manifest the fullness of what has been declared and established.

Job 22:28
You will also declare a thing,
And it will be established for you;
So light will shine on your ways.

Just like with construction projects, blueprints are a prerequisite to obtaining required permits. Permits are proof that the plan is in accordance with the regulations and permission has been granted to develop all that is included, the fullness of the blueprint. The contractor then takes the lead, and through insight and wisdom, builds according to the design. Every inspection along the way is judged in accordance to the blueprint.

Paul assures us in 2 Corinthians 8:10-12, all that is needed to begin *the* work is a willing mind and what is already in our hand. God does not expect us to do anything with what we do not have. God does expect us to do everything with what He has already given us – every gift, talent, like, dislike, agitation (which is an indication of the problem you have been sent as a solution to solve), resource, position, etc. God is looking for a return on His investment. Every provision for the vision is on the way to the vision.

---

2 Corinthians 8:10-12
And in this I give advice: It is to your advantage not only to be doing what you began and were desiring to do a year ago; but now you also must complete the doing of it; that as there was a readiness to desire it, so there also may be a completion out of what you have. For if there is first a willing mind, it is accepted according to what one has, and not according to what he does not have.

Psalm 119:105
Your word *is* a lamp to my feet
And a light to my path

Write unto the Lord

Flashlights, if attached to our feet, would only project light for a certain distance. In order to see further, we have to follow the Father. Advance! As you journey, with every step, the *light* you carry reveals more of what is ahead. Reflect: What is your next?

5

Delay

Pierced with Many Sorrows

For the love of money is a root of all *kinds* of evil, for which some have strayed from the faith in their greediness, and pierced themselves through with many sorrows.

1 Timothy 6:10

Showing a lack of remorse, Joseph's brothers sat down to eat while Joseph was in a nearby pit. Judah, who was Jacob's fourth son, born by Leah, said to his brothers in Genesis 37:26, "What profit is there if we kill our brother and conceal his blood?" He then divulged a plan to sell Joseph to the Ishmaelites.

And they sat down to eat a meal. Then they lifted their eyes and looked, and there was a company of Ishmaelites, coming from Gilead with their camels, bearing spices, balm, and myrrh, on their way to carry *them* down to Egypt. So Judah said to his brothers, "What profit *is there* if we kill our brother and conceal his blood? Come and let us sell him to the Ishmaelites, and let not our hand be upon him, for he is our brother *and* our flesh." And his brothers listened. Then Midianite traders passed by; so *the brothers* pulled Joseph up and lifted him out of the pit, and sold him to the Ishmaelites for twenty *shekels* of silver. And they took Joseph to Egypt.

Genesis 37:25-28

If there was no Ishmael there wouldn't have been any Ishmaelites to buy Joseph into slavery. Ishmael was a direct result of interference by man. At the age of seventy-five, it was prophetically announced by the Lord that Abram would be made "a great nation" and "to your descendants I will give this land" (*see* Genesis 12:1-7).

Reiterated again in Genesis 13:16 the Lord told Abram, "And I will make your descendants as the dust of the earth; so that if a man could number the dust of the earth, *then* your descendants also could be numbered." The promises the Lord declared, projected hundreds of years past Abram and Sarai's current childless circumstances.

After these things the word of the LORD came to Abram in a vision, saying, "Do not be afraid, Abram. *I am* your shield, your exceedingly great reward." But Abram said, "Lord GOD, what will You give me, seeing I go childless, and the heir of my house *is* Eliezer of Damascus?" Then Abram said, "Look, You have given me no offspring;

indeed one born in my house is my heir!" And behold, the word of the LORD *came* to him, saying, "This one shall not be your heir, but one who will come from your own body shall be your heir." Then He brought him outside and said, "Look now toward heaven, and count the stars if you are able to number them." And He said to him, "So shall your descendants be." And he believed in the LORD, and He accounted it to him for righteousness.

Genesis 15:1-6

Abram presented the possible option. Eliezer of Damascus was visible. He had already been born in Abram's house. The Lord presented the impossible option: one who will come from your own body shall be your heir. Isaac was invisible to Abram and Sarai; but already blueprinted by God as the child of promise. Isaac was divinely crafted by the Lord for a specific purpose and time to be released in the earth realm.

In Genesis 15:8 Abram asked, "Lord God, how shall I know that I will inherit it?" The Lord directed Abram to bring a very specific sacrificial offering. Abram did so and presented it in the customary arrangement.

And when the vultures came down on the carcasses, Abram drove them away. Now when the sun was going down, a deep sleep fell upon Abram; and behold, horror *and* great darkness fell upon him.

Genesis 15:11-12

The carcasses were dead and attracted consumers of death – vultures. Abram drove them away. At the first sign of life, the vultures had to flee. As long as there's breath in your body, beloved child of God, you are not a candidate for consumption.

Throughout Genesis 15, the Lord ministered to Abram and revealed to him insights centuries from his loins, when there was not one descendent yet in the earth. Even after such a great impartation, Sarai offered her Egyptian maidservant Hagar to Abram as an avenue to produce a child and Abram agreed to it (*see* Genesis 16:2). They tried to figure out a way to *help* God deliver His promise on their time schedule. They thought this was a *good* idea, but it was not the *right* idea and led to havoc in their family dynamics. Meanwhile, they still had to wait for the promise, while they dealt with the consequences of trying to do it their way.

> So he went in to Hagar, and she conceived. And when she saw that she had conceived, her mistress became despised in her eyes. Then Sarai said to Abram, "My wrong *be* upon you! I gave my maid into your embrace; and when she saw that she had conceived, I became despised in her eyes. The LORD judge between you and me."
>
> Genesis 16:4-5

Abram was eighty-six years old when Ishmael was born. The release of Isaac into the earth would come fourteen years later, when Abram was one hundred years old (*see* Genesis 21:5). In Genesis 17, Abram received the name Abraham (17:5) and Sarai received the name Sarah (17:15). Despite their interference, God's plan remained immovable, steadfast, and abounded.

> But My covenant I will establish with Isaac, whom Sarah shall bear to you at this set time next year.
>
> Genesis 17:21

> And the LORD visited Sarah as He had said, and the LORD did for Sarah as He had spoken. For Sarah conceived and bore Abraham a son in his old age, at the set time of which God had spoken to him. And Abraham called the name of his son who was born to him—whom Sarah bore to him—Isaac.
>
> Genesis 21:1-3

Every Seed Has a Voice

> And Sarah saw the son of Hagar the Egyptian, whom she had borne to Abraham, scoffing. Therefore she said to Abraham, "Cast out this bondwoman and her son; for the son of this bondwoman shall not be heir with my son, *namely* with Isaac." And the matter was very displeasing in Abraham's sight because of his son. But God said to Abraham, "Do not let it be displeasing in your sight because of the lad or because of your bondwoman. Whatever Sarah has said to you, listen to her voice; for in Isaac your seed shall be called. Yet I will also make a nation of the son of the bondwoman, because he *is* your seed."
>
> Genesis 21:9-13

Hagar and Ishmael, her now teenage son, were cast out because the cohabitation of the interference and the promise became increasingly more uncomfortable. Abraham gave them bread and a skin of water and sent them on their way to wander in the wilderness. The temporary supply of water Abraham gave them was used up and Hagar placed the boy under one of the shrubs and began to cry out (*see* Genesis 21:14-15).

> Then she [Hagar] went and sat down across from *him* [Ishmael] at a distance of about a bowshot; for she said to herself, "Let me not see the death of the boy." So she sat opposite *him*, and lifted her voice and wept. And God heard the voice of the lad. Then the angel of God called to Hagar out of heaven, and said to her, "What ails you, Hagar? Fear not, for God has heard the voice of the lad where he *is*. Arise, lift up the lad and hold him with your hand, for I will make him a great nation." Then God opened her eyes, and she saw a well of water. And she went and filled the skin with water, and gave the lad a drink. So God was with the lad; and he grew and dwelt in the wilderness, and became an archer.
>
> Genesis 21:16-20 (emphasis mine)

God heard the voice of the lad. The lad was the seed. Every seed has a voice. When man's provision depleted, God's provision was revealed.

At the beginning of Hagar's pregnancy, Sarai dealt harshly with her and Hagar fled into the wilderness (*see* Genesis 16:6-13). At that time, the Angel of the Lord spoke to her and sent her back to submit under Sarai. He also prophetically told her of the child, Ishmael, who was in her womb and gave her a glimpse of his destiny. Then she called the name of the Lord who spoke to her, *You-Are-the-God-Who-Sees*; for she said, "Have I also here seen Him who sees me?" (Genesis 16:13).

Hagar continually made tremendous sacrifices to remain obedient to Sarai and Abram; even yielding her body to bring forth Abram's child. Her obedience to the taskmaster caused her to become blind to her identity. Here in Genesis 21 is the day of Hagar's release from captivity, but she didn't see it yet. She had become so accustomed to the provision of the house of Abraham and Sarah, that she did not see the provision of the God of the House, until God opened her eyes to *see* the well of water (*see* Genesis 21:19). She then *went* and *filled* the skin with water and gave the lad a drink. Abraham's supply had been used up, but God's well erupted from an internal source which she was free to access again and again.

Notice the progression: Hagar *saw, went, filled,* and *gave*. These are all verbs. Hagar had to do to receive what was due! We live in a world full of prayers for the *nouns*: cars, houses, spouses, money, etc. Sentences are incomplete without verbs, just like the lives of Christians who draw back from doing the work of the word.

Gain Strength

Reflect on a few of the key prhases from this section:

❖ Cohabitation of the interference and the promise is uncomfortable.

❖ When man's provision is depleted, God's provision is revealed.

❖ Obedience to a wrongful taskmaster (harmful relationships, sickness, poverty, emotional turmoil, etc.) smothers one's identity.

❖ Becoming accustomed and bound to provision from a resource, can cause us to lose sight of the ultimate source.

❖ When the world's external supply runs dry, God's well will erupt from an internal source that we can freely access again and again.

❖ We must *do* to receive what is *due*.

❖ We live in a world full of prayers for the nouns: cars, houses, spouses, money, etc. Sentences are incomplete without verbs, just like the lives of Christians who draw back from doing the work of the word.

Write unto the Lord

Altered Evidence

Joseph was sold for twenty shekels of silver en route to Egypt. Reuben appeared to be absent during this transaction. The next time Reuben is spoken of is when he returned to the pit – as he previously planned to retrieve Joseph. Reuben found out his window of opportunity to make the situation right had passed; Joseph was not in the pit. Reuben failed to act with urgency and, as a result, found himself in greater turmoil.

> Then Reuben returned to the pit, and indeed Joseph was not in the pit; and he tore his clothes. And he returned to his brothers and said, "The lad *is* no *more*; and I, where shall I go?"
>
> Genesis 37:29-30

Evil begets evil and corruption begets corruption. After Joseph's brothers conspired and carried out their plan to get rid of Joseph, reality struck: What will they say to their father when his beloved son Joseph does not return home?

Joseph's brothers premeditated a scandal. They altered evidence to lead their father to the conclusion that Joseph was devoured by a wild beast.

> So they took Joseph's tunic, killed a kid of the goats, and dipped the tunic in the blood. Then they sent the tunic of *many* colors, and they brought *it* to their father and said, "We have found this. Do you know whether it is your son's tunic or not?" And he recognized it and said, "*It is* my son's tunic. A wild

beast has devoured him. Without doubt Joseph is torn to pieces." Then Jacob tore his clothes, put sackcloth on his waist, and mourned for his son many days. And all his sons and all his daughters arose to comfort him; but he refused to be comforted, and he said, "For I shall go down into the grave to my son in mourning." Thus his father wept for him. Now the Midianites had sold him in Egypt to Potiphar, an officer of Pharaoh *and* captain of the guard.

Genesis 37:31-36

After Joseph's brothers altered the evidence and presented it to their father as real, they asked a question to raise speculation: "Do you know whether it is your son's tunic or not?" Accepting this tampered evidence as real, Jacob validated that it was his son's tunic and his son must have been devoured by a wild beast and torn to pieces. With no further investigation, Jacob accepted death as his reality and refused to be comforted. The plan came together just as they concocted. Jacob bought the lie. He made a conclusion based on false evidence that appeared real.

Proverbs 3:25
Do not be afraid of sudden terror,
Nor of trouble from the wicked when it comes;

**G**ain **S**trength We must prepare ourselves ahead of time for sudden terror. Proverbs 3:25 says "when it comes" and directs our attention to our feet. Cross reference this scripture with Ephesians 6:15, "and having shod your feet with the preparation of the gospel of peace;" when dressing in the whole armor of God.

Ephesians 6:13
Therefore take up the whole armor of God,
that you may be able to withstand in the evil day,
and having done all, to stand.

The peace the world offers is defined by our circumstances, i.e. the expression, *no justice - no peace.* The gift of peace that Jesus gives us is not contingent upon any external factors. His peace is a prepared internal place that surpasses all human reasoning, henceforth, *know Jesus - know peace.* Peace is discussed more in Chapter 9 of this book.

A foundational confession, my pastor Errol Beckford has taught is, "We don't go by what it looks like. We don't go by what it feels like. We go by what the word of God says."

The devil wants you to picture your departure more than envisioning your life.

Have you made assumptions based on altered evidence? I know I have. Use this space to reflect.

Write unto the Lord

6

Destiny

Vision Helper

A seed has everything in it necessary for life. A seed can sit dormant for decades and never produce. A seed must be sown - committed to the darkness of the ground. In pursuit of water and light, the seed germinates, breaking free from the limitations of the outer covering. Plants have an inherited automaticity to grow in the direction of light.

Purchased as a slave, Joseph entered the house of Potiphar in Egypt. He refused to allow his current level to limit him. As does the seed, Joseph had every God-given thing in himself necessary for life and chose to grow in the direction of the light, escaping the darkness.

Now Joseph had been taken down to Egypt. And Potiphar, an officer of Pharaoh, captain of the guard, an Egyptian, bought him from the Ishmaelites who had taken him down there. The LORD was with Joseph, and he was a successful man; and he was in the house of his master the Egyptian. And his master saw that the LORD *was* with him and that the LORD made all he did to prosper in his hand. So Joseph found favor in his sight, and served him. Then he made him overseer of his house, and all *that* he had he put under his authority. So it was, from the *time* that he had made him overseer of his house and all that he had, that the LORD blessed the Egyptian's house for Joseph's sake; and the blessing of the LORD was on all that he had in the house and in the field. Thus he left all that he had in Joseph's hand, and he did not know what he had except for the bread which he ate. Now Joseph was handsome in form and appearance.

Genesis 39:1-6

Joseph's current circumstances did not match the dreams God had given him; but he was committed to fully engage and practice the gifts that God entrusted him with by being a vision helper to Potiphar. Despite what we think of certain authority figures, all authority is from God and we are directed to submit.

Let every soul be subject to the governing authorities. For there is no authority except from God, and the authorities that exist are appointed by God.

Romans 13:1

The Lord blessed the Egyptian's house for Joseph's sake; and the blessing of the Lord was on all that he (Potiphar) had in the house and in the field. Joseph could have found entitlement in disappointment and bitterness. Instead, he purposefully chose obedience, and allowed God's principles to prevail. Whose Joseph are you? Who is blessed *because* you are there doing all things unto the Lord?

> And whatever you do, do it heartily, as to the Lord and not to men, knowing that from the Lord you will receive the reward of the inheritance; for you serve the Lord Christ.
>
> Colossians 3:23-24

The Lord Jesus Christ is our ultimate authority and as we do all things unto Him, we receive access to the reward of *the* inheritance. With God, there is *one* inheritance. It is disbursed in two installments: an earthly installment and a heavenly installment.

We are sent into this earth to rule, His reward is with Him, and His work is before Him. As His arm, we are to extend our faith and His authority, to bring forth demonstrations of power by His strong hand. Think about it. Our arms allow the full potential and purpose of our hands to be maximized. Isaiah 40:10 proclaims, "Behold, the Lord God shall come with a strong *hand*, And His arm shall rule for Him; Behold, His reward is with Him, And His work before Him."

Gain Strength

A dirty seed, covered with the weight of the earth, is in position to establish a foundation. A clean seed, displayed on the most expensive shelf, is not in position to establish a foundation and its potential will remain dormant.

Science tells us that seeds are dispersed in multiple ways, to include: water or wind; heat causing pods to burst; and by birds and animals consuming them then later releasing the seeds within their *droppings*. The water, wind, heat, consumers, and even the times you have dealt with the *droppings of life*, have all led you to the place you are now on your journey.

Write unto the Lord

What gift, talent, idea, resource, etc. do you need to sow in order to grow?

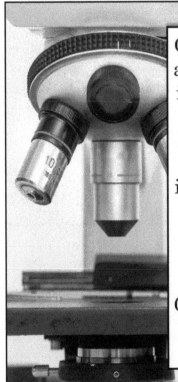

God is not **inspecting** all of our wrongs. God is **expecting** a return on all of our *rights*. Every *right* thing He has embedded and intertwined within us and every *right* He has awarded to us through the shed blood of Jesus Christ—the authority, backing, & resources of heaven.

7

Deterred

The Net is Cast

Looking back into the lineage of Joseph, we see that he came from a line of men who had children with multiple women. Jacob, his father, had a total of thirteen named children from four women. Abraham, his great-grandfather had Ishmael by Hagar, Isaac by Sarah, then six more sons by his wife Keturah - after the death of Sarah (*see* Genesis 25:1-2). It is also noted in Genesis 25:6, "Abraham gave gifts to the sons of the concubines which Abraham had."

Joseph had first-hand experience of the chaos which can arise living in a home consisting of half-brothers and their mothers. Knowing what he did *not* want pushed Joseph into what he *did* want.

Joseph was physically handsome in form and appearance. The Lord made all he did to prosper in his hand. He was a great administrator in Potiphar's house. Joseph was entrusted with all Potiphar had. The only thing Potiphar was concerned with was "the bread which he ate," (*see* Genesis 39:6).

The physical build of Joseph's body, his looks, gifting, work ethic, and the elevation on his life were attractive to Potiphar's wife and day by day she executed a regimen of seduction.

> And it came to pass after these things that his master's wife cast longing eyes on Joseph, and she said, "Lie with me." But he refused and said to his master's wife, "Look, my master does not know what is with me in the house, and he has committed all that he has to my hand. *There is* no one greater in this house than I, nor has he kept back anything from me but you, because you *are* his wife. How then can I do this great wickedness, and sin against God?" So it was, as she spoke to Joseph day by day, that he did not heed her, to lie with her *or* to be with her.
>
> Genesis 39:7-10

Joseph valued righteousness. He recognized, that above all, he would be transgressing against God if he were to take the given opportunities to lie with Potiphar's wife. Day by day, Joseph continually renewed his mind to stand firm against the ever-present temptation of sexual immorality. Joseph recognized how truly valuable he was and to Whom he ultimately belonged, stating, "There is no one greater in this house than I," and, "If I do this great wickedness it would be sin against God" (*see* Genesis 39:9). The net was cast but Joseph remained obedient proving Psalm 25:15, "My eyes are ever toward the Lord, For He shall pluck my feet out of the net."

Joseph had the assurance that God was not limiting him. Boundaries are instilled to protect. Potiphar's wife was for Potiphar. We are called to be faithful in what is another man's in order to get our own, as reasoned in Luke 16:12, "And if you have not been faithful in what is another man's, who will give you what is your own?"

Joseph abided in this principle. He was a vision helper to Potiphar, although he entered the house as a slave, he gained authority over the house. Over time, Joseph was further elevated by God and declared by Pharaoh, who is higher ranking than Potiphar, to a set position over all the land of Egypt (*see* Genesis 41:41). Joseph was commissioned to administer the plan that God gave him to preserve Egypt and surrounding nations during the time of famine.

Joseph's refusal to transgress against the marriage covenant preserved Joseph until the set time of which he was given Pharaoh's daughter, Asenath, as wife, who bore him two sons (*see* Genesis 46:20). The barrenness of the previous generations: of Sarah (Abraham his great-grandfather); Rebekah (Isaac his grandfather); and Rachel (Jacob his father), were not Asenath and Joseph's portion.

Joseph saw Ephraim's children to the third generation. The children of Machir, the son of Manasseh, were also brought up on Joseph's knees.

Genesis 50:23

FLEE Sexual Immorality

Joseph did not have a modern-day, signed, written contract with God stating, "If you do right by Potiphar as a slave in his house, I will set you over all the land of Egypt, reunite you with your blood family, and give seventy-plus members of your family the goodness of Goshen," nor stating, "If you refuse Potiphar's wife, I will give you Asenath for a wife - who has a fruitful womb." Joseph had two dreams as a seventeen-year-old boy that caused his brothers to hate him even more, and his father to rebuke him: some non-examples of what he did not want in his life; and one faithful God, whom he chose to honor, proving obedience overcomes obstacles.

Joseph denied Potiphar's wife day after day, but one day at an opportune time, she got close enough to catch him by his garment.

> But it happened about this time, when Joseph went into the house to do his work, and none of the men of the house *was* inside, that she caught him by his garment, saying, "Lie with me." But he left his garment in her hand, and fled and ran outside.
>
> Genesis 39:11-12

Joseph did exactly what the Bible instructs us to do when it comes to sexual immorality - and that is to *flee*. Sexual immorality is sin against one's own body. There are physical consequences of sexual immorality that take place in the body, such as sexually transmitted diseases. There are also emotional consequences that take place in the mind and the heart that often leave lifelong scars. Likewise, there are spiritual transactions that take place as two become one flesh, giving each body access to the other's entanglements and strongholds.

Flee sexual immorality. Every sin that a man does is outside the body, but he who commits sexual immorality sins against his own body.

1 Corinthians 6:18

 As we journey through life, often the list of what we don't want grows longer and the list of what we do want becomes shorter. This happens as we find out, the things we once thought were appealing, bring no lasting fulfillment. We tend to then refocus on the age-old question, "What is the purpose of life?" And more specifically, "What is the purpose of *my* life?"

Isaiah 60:8
"Who *are* these *who* fly like a cloud,
And like doves to their roosts?[']

Ephesians 1:20-23
which He worked in Christ when He raised Him from the dead and seated *Him* at His right hand in the heavenly *places,* far above all principality and power and might and dominion, and every name that is named,
not only in this age but also in that which is to come.
And He put all *things* under His feet, and gave Him *to be* head over all *things* to the church, which is His body, the fullness of Him who fills all in all.

With the ariel view, mentioned in Isaiah 60:8 and Ephesians 1:20-23, we are able to see the course of our journey. We are able to see ways of escape during times of temptation, distraction, or turmoil; are privy to snares and demonic conspiracies; and we can clearly identify routes of opportunity, advancement, elevation, and distinction.

Like a dove to its roost, there is a niche in the vastness of the world, for every dove, just as there is a mandate for each of us to locate for our life. Think about all the greenery throughout the earth and how similar it looks. A dove has divine direction to return to the roost *they* made the investment to build.

Disciples are *disciplined ones.* In life, we must mature to the point that we are able to discipline ourselves. If we don't discipline ourselves, someone else will always have to - our boss, teacher, law enforcement, a family member, or even a spouse.

When we focus on doing the *dos*, we don't have time for the *don'ts*.

1 Corinthians 13:11
When I was a child, I spoke as a child, I understood as a child, I thought as a child; but when I became a man, I put away childish things.

Hebrews 5:8
[T]hough He was a Son, *yet* He learned obedience by the things which He suffered.

Develop What is *Right* for You

Write unto the **Lord** Luke 16:12 reminds us, "And if you have not been faithful in what is another man's, who will give you what is your own?" Celebrate your progress so far and know your faithfulness over the little qualifies you to be a ruler over much.

_____

_____

_____

_____

_____

_____

_____

_____

_____

_____

_____

_____

_____

_____

_____

_____

_____

_____

_____

8

Designed

Vision

Vision was created first and then each person was designed, even to their most inward parts; equipped to manifest the vision from which they were created. Do you find yourself asking, *Lord, why me?* The answer is, because it had to be you. You were designed for the vision; the vision was not designed for you. The vision was created first and then the person was created to manifest the vision into the earth. Some scriptures accentuating this are:

Before I formed you in the womb I knew you; Before you were born I sanctified you; I ordained you a prophet to the nations.

Jeremiah 1:5

For I know the thoughts that I think toward you, says the Lord, thoughts of peace and not of evil, to give you a future and a hope.

Jeremiah 29:11

For You formed my inward parts; You covered me in my mother's womb. I will praise You, for I am fearfully *and* wonderfully made; Marvelous are Your works, And *that* my soul knows very well. My frame was not hidden from You, When I was made in secret, *And* skillfully wrought in the lowest parts of the earth. Your eyes saw my substance, being yet unformed. And in Your book they all were written, The days fashioned for me, When *as yet there were* none of them.

Psalm 139:13-16

The Bible tells us of proclamations made, some even before conception, of mighty men who arrived in the earth on divine assignment, through the womb of women previously called barren.

God to Abraham (Sarah) before Isaac was conceived:

Then God said: "No, Sarah your wife shall bear you a son, and you shall call his name Isaac; I will establish My covenant with him for an everlasting covenant, and with his descendants after him."

Genesis 17:19

But My covenant I will establish with Isaac, whom Sarah shall bear to you at this set time next year.

Genesis 17:21

The Lord to Rebekah (Isaac) while the twins Esau & Jacob were in her womb:

And the Lord said to her: "Two nations are in your womb, Two peoples shall be separated from your body; One people shall be stronger than the other, And the older shall serve the younger."

Genesis 25:23

God remembered Rachel (Jacob) and opened her womb:

Then God remembered Rachel, and God listened to her and opened her womb. And she conceived and bore a son, and said, "God has taken away my reproach."

Genesis 30:22-23

Angel of the Lord to an unnamed woman (Manoah) before Samson was conceived:

And the Angel of the Lord appeared to the woman and said to her, "Indeed now, you are barren and have borne no children, but you shall conceive and bear a son."

Judges 13:3

Eli to Hannah (Elkanah) before Samuel was conceived:

Then Eli answered and said, "Go in peace, and the God of Israel grant your petition which you have asked of Him."

1 Samuel 1:17

So it came to pass in the process of time that Hannah conceived and bore a son, and called his name Samuel, saying, "Because I have asked for him from the Lord."

1 Samuel 1:20

Angel to Zacharias (Elizabeth) before
John the Baptist was conceived:

But the angel said to him, "Do not be afraid, Zacharias, for your prayer is heard; and your wife Elizabeth will bear you a son, and you shall call his name John."

Luke 1:13

Mary was never called barren, but was a virgin.
Conception took place at the word!

And behold, you will conceive in your womb and bring forth a Son, and shall call His name Jesus.

Luke 1:31

These scriptures bring repeated confirmation of the significance and uniqueness of each person's precious life! The vision is viable! In the words of our Lord Jesus Christ, "With men this is impossible, but with God all things are possible" (Matthew 19:26).

Gain Strength Revelation of the covenant of life is contrary to the customary marking on a tombstone, which shows a linear perception of life, with a starting point (birthdate), a dash representing time, and an endpoint (date of death). In this manner, time is marked by the chronological calendar of the earth. God is outside of time. He is Sovereign. People sometimes say, "God may not come when you want Him, but He sure comes when you need Him - in the midnight hour," or what we perceive as the last possible opportunity. God is from everlasting to everlasting. He knows the beginning from the end. In most situations we only know the right now and past experiences.

Like Hagar, we must trust, the God who sees us. The One who authored the vision for our life in the books of heaven.

Reflect on your journey so far. How have, at first seemingly different parts of your life, now come together to form a greater picture? **Write unto the Lord**

Altered Evidence (again)

Joseph operated in integrity and denied the repeated advances of Potiphar's wife. As he fled one day, the hand of the seductress captured his garment. For the second time noted, an enemy in possession of Joseph's garment, altered the evidence in an attempt to alter Joseph's destiny. Potiphar's wife brought a false accusation against Joseph.

> And so it was, when she saw that he had left his garment in her hand and fled outside, that she called to the men of her house and spoke to them, saying, "See, he has brought in to us a Hebrew to mock us. He came in to me to lie with me, and I cried out with a loud voice. And it happened, when he heard that I lifted my voice and cried out, that he left his garment with me, and fled and went outside." So she kept his garment with her until his master came home. Then she spoke to him with words like these, saying, "The Hebrew servant whom you brought to us came in to me to mock me; so it happened, as I lifted my voice and cried out, that he left his garment with me and fled outside." So it was, when his master heard the words which his wife spoke to him, saying, "Your servant did to me after this manner," that his anger was aroused. Then Joseph's master took him and put him into the prison, a place where the king's prisoners *were* confined. And he was there in the prison.
>
> Genesis 39:13-20

Fruit of the Spirit

Joseph produced much fruit in Potiphar's house. In the seed cycle, fruit is produced around the seed to protect and nourish it. We know that the word of God is the seed (*see* Luke 8:11). In Galatians 5:22-23 we are introduced to the fruits of the Spirit which are love, joy, peace, longsuffering, kindness, goodness, faithfulness, gentle-ness, and self-control. Ephesians 5:9 expounds further by stating, "for the fruit of the Spirit *is* in all goodness, righteousness, and truth." When we choose to operate in the fruits of the Spirit, we protect the seed of the word within us.

In time, ripe fruit, if not harvested, will drop from the vine and be committed to the ground to fertilize and replenish. This is why we can't allow ourselves to be paralyzed by disappointment when we are not *harvested* by others on the timeline we set for ourselves.

Trust God's hand of elevation and God's timing. Never cease cultivating your gifts. Do all things wholeheartedly as unto the Lord. When dropped, we must embed ourselves back into the good ground. The ground is good where one is doing the work of the word.

The Parable of the Sower

And as he sowed, some *seed* fell by the wayside; and the birds came and devoured them. Some fell on stony places, where they did not have much earth; and they immediately sprang up because they had no depth of earth. But when the sun was up they were scorched, and because they had no root they withered away. And some fell among thorns, and the thorns sprang up and choked them. But others fell on good ground and yielded a crop: some a hundredfold, some sixty, some thirty.

Matthew 13:4-8

In all four scenarios, there is nothing wrong with the seed! It's the landing point of the seed that makes the difference. Seed on the wayside can be moved to good ground by wind, representing the breath of God; or rain, representing the water of the word.

Stones or obstacles can be removed and earth can be added to make a way for the seed:

Go through, Go through the gates! Prepare the way for the people; Build up, Build up the highway! Take out the stones, Lift up a banner for the peoples!

Isaiah 62:10

I will give you a new heart and put a new spirit within you; I will take the heart of stone out of your flesh and give you a heart of flesh.

Ezekiel 36:26

Thorny vines can be rooted out, pulled down, destroyed, and thrown down to clear ground for the seed to take dominion:

Behold, I have put My words in your mouth. See, I have this day set you over the nations and over the kingdoms, To root out and to pull down, To destroy and to throw down, To build and to plant.

Jeremiah 1:9-10

Prioritize the Vision

Good ground can be created through clearing, plowing, tilling, cultivating, and fertilizing! Joseph found himself committed to the ground of the prison cell. He did not interpret this as the end but allowed himself to be pliable clay in the hands of the Master Potter.

> And the vessel that he made of clay was marred in the hand of the potter; so he made it again into another vessel, as it seemed good to the potter to make. Then the word of the LORD came to me, saying: "O house of Israel, can I not do with you as this potter?" says the LORD. "Look, as the clay *is* in the potter's hand, so *are* you in My hand, O house of Israel!

> Jeremiah 18:4-6

Knowing that although the circumstances changed, His God remained the same, Joseph continued to prioritize the vision by practicing and cultivating his God-given giftings and talents in the prison.

> But the LORD was with Joseph and showed him mercy, and He gave him favor in the sight of the keeper of the prison. And the keeper of the prison committed to Joseph's hand all the prisoners who *were* in the prison; whatever they did there, it was

his doing. The keeper of the prison did not look into anything *that was* under *Joseph's* authority, because the LORD was with him; and whatever he did, the LORD made it prosper.

Genesis 39:21-23

When we choose to honor God in all we do, keep the word of God in our mouth, meditate in it day and night, and do it as it is written, we make our way prosperous and produce good success.

This Book of the Law shall not depart from your mouth, but you shall meditate in it day and night, that you may observe to do according to all that is written in it. For then you will make your way prosperous, and then you will have good success.

Joshua 1:8

Ideas

In the *Parable of the Sower*, the farmer who went out to sow had a good ground destination to develop his seed. We know the seed *is* the word of God. Combining that principle with John 1:3, "All things were made through Him, and without Him nothing was made that was made," we can extract the revelation *ideas* are seeds.

Every good gift and every perfect gift is from above, and comes down from the Father of lights, with whom there is no variation or shadow of turning.

James 1:17

The devil has no creative power. Wickedness is a result of God's good and perfect idea being twisted by the evil desires of an impure heart.

❖ Sex is God's good design for the marriage covenant. When corrupted and accessed outside of God's intention, ungodly sexual acts have brought continuous turbulence, turmoil, and torment to people, lingering long past the physical act.

❖ All precious wealth (gold, gemstones, etc.) were created within the earth by God's design. He is Lord over all. However, the *love* of money is noted as being the root of all *kinds of* evil, although wealth itself is not evil, but necessary (*see* 1 Timothy 6:10).

❖ Natural remedies are found in the earth for ailments and disease, as well as health and wellness. God created them good to solve problems before they even existed. Corruption has altered, chemicalized, and redirected the original intent of these substances resulting in many people being overtaken by drug addiction. The harmful consequences are extended to their family, friends, community, and the totality of society.

Original God-given ideas have a good ground destination. Ideas that fall by the *wayside* are those we do not act on. They burn up or are devoured. Ideas that fall in the *stony ground* are the ones we act on initially with excitement but give up on when the results do not come as fast or easy as we expected. Ideas that fall in the *thorny ground* are the ones that we have dedicated significant time, energy, money, and resources into. We have sacrificed and invested yet remain frustrated because *it* has not yet become financially profitable. Jesus said, the *cares of this world* choke out the seed. Money is a primary care of this world. It has been said, *prayer moves heaven and money moves the earth.*

My husband and I have a saying, "Until a business is profitable, it is a hobby." While both of our businesses were still in the *hobby* stage, we made a quality decision, to persevere much over the years and stay the course. Overtime, both businesses have moved forward. An encouraging expression our pastor uses is, "Keep knocking at the well."

Notice the location of the thorny ground. It is the adjacent piece of property on the outskirts of the good ground. The good ground is the place of the thirty, sixty, and hundredfold return.

Proverbs 18:16
A man's gift makes room for him,
And brings him before great men.

Gain Strength

God asked Adam two profound questions in Genesis chapter 3: "Where *are* you?" And, "Who told you that you *were* naked?"

Reflect on these questions. Where *are* you? On the wayside, stony ground, among the thorns, or bountifully producing good ground?

Write unto the Lord

Who told you that you *were* naked? What voice is telling you that what you have is inadequate and needs to be hidden – keeping you in a place of limitation?

9

Desire

Choose a Pure Mind

With a corrupt mind comes terror of every sort. A corrupt mind constantly questions the intentions of others. It meditates on every possible scenario to negate ideas, opportunities, relationships, etc. It plots to reject authority in word and deed.

In Joseph's life, he exhibited purity. A corrupt mind would have justified giving up or revolting against authority, or working toward unjust gain. Joseph didn't do any of these things because he *chose* purity.

> To the pure all things are pure, but to those who are defiled and unbelieving nothing is pure; but even their mind and conscience are defiled. They profess to know God, but in works they deny *Him*, being abominable, disobedient, and disqualified for every good work.
>
> Titus 1:15-16

A pure mind ceases raging fickle feelings. Choosing God's guiding foundational principles and moving on His word is the avenue of deliverance from chaotic circumstances, even when the circumstances don't go away.

Obedience Fortifies Us

Obedience fortifies us; while disobedience forfeits us. Jesus said in John 14:15, "If you love Me, keep My commandments," and in John 14:24, "He who does not love Me does not keep My words; and the word which you hear is not Mine but the Father's who sent Me." In James 1:21-22 we are directed to, "...lay aside all filthiness and overflow of wickedness, and receive with meekness the implanted word, which is able to save your souls. But be doers of the word, and not hearers only, deceiving yourselves."

In James 1:25, *doer of the word* is transposed with *doer of the work,* "... and is not a forgetful hearer but a doer of the work, this one will be blessed in what he does." As emphasized, the one who obediently performs the work of the word will be blessed!

Operating in the Midst of Enemies

Throughout the Old Testament, there are two types of deliverance from enemies noted: deliverance out of the hand of the enemy, and the deliverance of the enemy into the hand of the righteous. Either way, the ability to operate in the midst of enemies is essential for elevation.

Enemies have no authority over a blood-bought royal son or daughter of God. They are merely an intimidation tactic assigned to kindle fear and inferiority. The New Testament notes, there is an enemy at work but the ransom has already been paid for deliverance. There is repeated instruction to love and forgive enemies in word and deed. Moreover, the New Testament teaches of the victorious position we possess through Christ Jesus that supersedes every enemy.

ANGER

Be angry, and do not sin. Meditate within your heart on your bed, and be still. Selah Offer the sacrifices of righteousness, And put your trust in the Lord.

Psalm 4:4-5

Anger is an emotion that rises, but in anger do not sin. *Meditate within your heart* (spirit) *on your bed and be still.* A *bed* is more than something to sleep on. A bed is also a place of life and growth, i.e. *flower* bed or *oyster* bed.

Anger is a warning sign that something is not right in a situation. Anger also reveals areas within us needing to be addressed. Offering sacrifices of righteousness means to let go of the ungodly response in exchange for a godly response and solution to the situation.

When a person delights in the Lord, He gives them the desires of their heart. That does not mean God *lets people have their way.* It means that as a person delights in Him, He puts *His desires* into their heart, returning it to the original design! Trust in the Lord! *Let Go and Let God!*

Trust in the Lord, and do good; Dwell in the land, and feed on His faithfulness. Delight yourself also in the Lord, And He shall give you the desires of your heart. Commit your way to the Lord, Trust also in Him, And He shall bring *it* to pass.

Psalm 37:3-5

Renewing the Mind

The enemy works to alienate people through their minds by wicked works. This type of *wickedness* is usually subtle. A *wick* is a porous absorbent material. Twisted or woven items are known as wicker. Knowing the mind is a fertile place, the enemy strategically works to twist and turn the mind away from the light of the truth of God to darkness through suggestions like: *what if; it's not going to work; you can't do that; you're not worthy; you will never get better;* etc.

The truth is, not only was the blood of Jesus shed for the forgiveness of all sin once and for all; but it was also shed for the cleansing of the conscience from dead works to serve the living God. Apply the blood of Jesus to cleanse your conscience from dead works, which includes tormenting perverse images of past experiences.

And you, who once were alienated and enemies in your mind by wicked works, yet now He has reconciled in the body of His flesh through death, to present you holy, and blameless, and above reproach in His sight—

Colossians 1:21-22

> [H]ow much more shall the blood of Christ, who through the eternal Spirit offered Himself without spot to God, cleanse your conscience from dead works to serve the living God?
>
> Hebrews 9:14

Authorization to possess the mind of Christ has been given to all born again believers. Paul asserts in Philippians 2:5, "Let this mind be in you which was also in Christ Jesus." The word *let* is a directive for us to allow the mind of Christ Jesus to subdue the natural and carnal mind, so the spiritual mind can reign. This is done through obedience to the strategic plan of God for mind transformation.

> [C]asting down arguments and every high thing that exalts itself against the knowledge of God, bringing every thought into captivity to the obedience of Christ, and being ready to punish all disobedience when your obedience is fulfilled.
>
> 2 Corinthians 10:5-6

The enemy works to deposit contraceptives into the powerful womb of the mind so Godly seeds do not conceive. To cast down arguments and every high thing that exalts itself against the knowledge of God means to evict negative and destructive imaginations that arise to cause confusion, insecurity, anxiety, clouded thinking, and every other terror. Every thought must be brought into captivity to the obedience of Christ by purposely directing meditations of the mind and confessions of the mouth, which become the condition of the heart.

Only refusing to think about something leaves vast open space in the mind for even worse thoughts to swarm. Seeds of the word must be sown in the mind. As the word of God firmly roots, it establishes dominion. The mind transforms into an arsenal ready to punish all disobedience when obedience has been fulfilled.

The Holy Spirit is our teacher and brings the word of God into remembrance to slay every contrary thought trying to invade the mind. Throughout the Gospels, Jesus repeatedly introduced the Holy Spirit and all His benefits. For instance, Jesus taught in John 14:26, "But the Helper, the Holy Spirit, whom the Father will send in My name, He will teach you all things, and bring to your remembrance all things that I said to you."

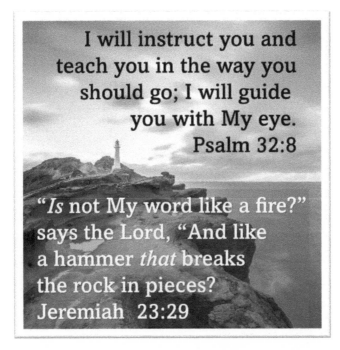

I will instruct you and teach you in the way you should go; I will guide you with My eye.
Psalm 32:8

"*Is* not My word like a fire?" says the Lord, "And like a hammer *that* breaks the rock in pieces?
Jeremiah 23:29

Write unto the **Lord**

Identify a negative script that continually presents itself in your mind in an attempt to weaken you on your journey. Cast it down and apply the blood of Jesus to your conscience. Seek God's word to guide you.

PEACE

In the book of Philippians, Paul provides the recipe for peace that surpasses all understanding, which is assigned to guard our hearts and minds.

> Be anxious for nothing, but in everything by prayer and supplication, with thanksgiving, let your requests be made known to God; and the peace of God, which surpasses all understanding, will guard your hearts and minds through Christ Jesus. Finally, brethren, whatever things are true, whatever things *are* noble, whatever things *are* just, whatever things *are* pure, whatever things *are* lovely, whatever things *are* of good report, if *there is* any virtue and if *there is* anything praiseworthy—meditate on these things. The things which you learned and received and heard and saw in me, these do, and the God of peace will be with you.
>
> Philippians 4:6-9

Paul's life is a testimony of the power of the transformed mind and the ability to operate in peace regardless of one's past. The Lord spoke to Ananias in Acts 9:15 and identified Paul as, "a chosen vessel of Mine to bear My name." Paul boldly established the kingdom of God, with the centerpiece being Jesus Christ.

Prior to his conversion, Paul's name was Saul. Saul destroyed, even to death, as many people as he could who were following the teachings of Christ before he exited the camp of darkness. When light comes, it voids darkness of its power. "But you *are* a chosen generation, a royal priesthood, a holy nation, His own special people, that you may proclaim the praises of Him who called you out of darkness into His marvelous light;" (1 Peter 2:9).

Today, Paul is known for his epistles throughout the New Testament; focusing on transforming the mind, sharing his testimony, encouraging believers, enduring hardships, and expounding on the teachings of Jesus Christ, who he knew personally through revelation.

Generate a Harvest

If something is not true, then it is not for you. If something is *not* noble, just, pure, nor lovely; do not allow it to spawn in your mind. Fill your mind and your mouth with meditations and confessions focusing on things that are true, noble, just, pure, lovely, of good report, virtuous, and praiseworthy to manifest the peace of God which only comes from the God of peace!

A wise farmer sows seeds compatible with the environment and seasons. Purposefully and carefully select the seeds of your meditation which are sown through the confessions of your mouth. As natural seeds take dominion of the piece of land they are sown in, so is it in your mind. Strategically sow for your desired harvest.

Sow and sew are homophones. The word sew means to join, fasten, or repair. Positive seeds repair by *sewing* tears within us; the holes and shattered pieces. They also uproot and replace sown tares choking the desired harvest. The meditations and confessions we sow, join and fasten with good or bad forces to produce what we say.

> Day unto day utters speech, and night unto night reveals knowledge. *There is* no speech nor language where their voice is not heard. Their line has gone out through all the earth, and their words to the end of the world...
>
> Psalm 19:2-4

Mind Transformation

Mind transformation is the greatest miracle that has taken place in my life. The power to void plaguing destructive thinking patterns is readily available. Application of the principles found in God's word is essential and they work for those who work them!

> I beseech you therefore, brethren, by the mercies of God, that you present your bodies a living sacrifice, holy, acceptable to God, *which* is your reasonable service. And do not be conformed to this world, but be transformed by the renewing of your mind, that you may prove what is that good and acceptable and perfect will of God.
>
> Romans 12:1-2

> Who remembered us in our lowly state, For His mercy *endures* forever; And rescued us from our enemies, For His mercy *endures* forever; Who gives food to all flesh, For His mercy *endures* forever. Oh, give thanks to the God of heaven! For His mercy endures forever.
>
> Psalm 136:23-26

To beseech is to cry out with great desire for someone to hear and benefit from the words coming next. When we were caught up in the very act of the worst things we have ever done, it was God who saw past that moment of time, *our lowly state*, and extended His mercy unto us.

In honor of His mercy, choose to present your body, mind, and spirit as a living sacrifice; holy and acceptable to God. *Conformed* means to take the shape of the surroundings, as liquid does when it is poured from container to container. You are called to be *transformed* by the renewing of your mind. The transformed mind is a weapon of warfare that makes you, "steadfast, immovable, always abounding in the work of the Lord, knowing that your labor is not in vain in the Lord" (1 Corinthians 15:58).

Christ desires your mind to be identifiably transformed for your sake and for His. In the doing of the work of the word, you prove what is *that* good, acceptable, and perfect will of God.

Combining the many people, influences, and life experiences that mold our minds with spiritual fiery darts of the wicked one, no wonder people are desperately seeking mind alteration. All these factors, however, are not responsible for the corruption of the mind. What *we* allow to breed in the inner man leads to defilement. Jesus taught in Mark 7:15, "There is nothing that enters a man from outside which can defile him; but the things which come out of him, those are the things that defile a man." Output is created by thoughts meditated on, that become feelings, then behavior.

The power of the Holy Spirit delights in working through you to produce exceedingly, abundantly above all that you ask or think. Operate in full confidence and establish the vision God sent you into the earth to manifest for His Glory, the benefit of His people, and to activate the power He has given you to get wealth. In Jesus Name.

> Now to Him who is able to do exceedingly abundantly above all that we ask or think, according to the power that works in us, to Him *be* glory in the church by Christ Jesus to all generations, forever and ever. Amen.
>
> Ephesians 3:20-21

> "And you shall remember the LORD your God, for *it is* He who gives you power to get wealth, that He may establish His covenant which He swore to your fathers, as *it is* this day.
>
> Deuteronomy 8:18

Gain Strength

Our thoughts determine how we feel. Our feelings manifest into behavior. And our behaviors form our days, weeks, months, years, and life.

What are some thoughts you *must* cast down and what are some of the thoughts you *must* intentionally add to your thinking pattern in order to

Write unto the Lord

experience the peace that surpasses all understanding and human reasoning? Intentionally targeting our thoughts strengthens us for our journey.

....

....

....

....

....

....

....

....

....

....

....

....

....

....

....

....

10

Diligence

Persevere Under Duress

Persevere! *Per* means to divide. *Sever* means to remove by cutting or force. *Severe* means great intensity. To *persevere* means to diligently work to separate the desired foreseen result from every opposing force. In Potiphar's house and in the prison, Joseph persevered as he continued to operate in his God-given giftings under duress, which melted the power of the enemy!

> It came to pass after these things *that* the butler and the baker of the king of Egypt offended their lord, the king of Egypt. And Pharaoh was angry with his two officers, the chief butler and the chief baker. So he put them in custody in the house of the captain of the guard, in the prison, the place where Joseph *was* confined. And the captain of the guard charged Joseph with them, and he served them; so they were in custody for a while. Then the butler and the baker of the king of Egypt, who *were* confined in the prison, had a dream, both of them, each man's dream in one night *and* each man's dream with its *own* interpretation. And Joseph

came in to them in the morning and looked at them, and saw that they *were* sad. So he asked Pharaoh's officers who *were* with him in the custody of his lord's house, saying, "Why do you look *so* sad today?" And they said to him, "We each have had a dream, and *there* is no interpreter of it." So Joseph said to them, "Do not interpretations belong to God? Tell *them* to me, please."

Genesis 40:1-8

Joseph accurately interpreted the dreams of both the butler and the baker. The butler was given a word of restoration, but the fate of the baker would be death. Joseph petitioned the butler in Genesis 40:14, "But remember me when it is well with you, and please show kindness to me; make mention of me to Pharaoh, and get me out of this house."

The butler was restored and did not make mention of Joseph to Pharaoh for two whole years. Thankfully, God is not a man, therefore He cannot lie and remained faithful to Joseph when he was forgotten by the butler.

In lieu of allowing disappointment to set in, Joseph kept practicing his God-given gift of administration in the prison as a vision helper to the keeper of the prison.

Pharaoh had dreams that troubled his spirit. Pharaoh called for all the magicians of Egypt and all its wise men, but they were unable to interpret his dreams (*see* Genesis 41:8). Suddenly, at the opportune time, probably thinking he might gain stature for himself, the butler made mention of Joseph to Pharaoh.

Now there *was* a young Hebrew man with us there, a servant of the captain of the guard. And we told him, and he interpreted our dreams for us; to each man he interpreted according to his *own* dream. And it came to pass, just as he interpreted for us, so it happened. He restored me to my office, and he hanged him." Then Pharaoh sent and called Joseph, and they brought him quickly out of the dungeon; and he shaved, changed his clothing, and came to Pharaoh.

Genesis 41:12-14

Joseph was shaved. This removed the appearance of time and signified the redemption of time. His clothes were changed; the chaff shed for the harvest. Joseph was thirty years old when he stood before Pharaoh; thirteen years after being sold into Egypt as a slave.

Joseph's life is proof of Proverbs 22:29, "Do you see a man *who* excels in his work? He will stand before kings; He will not stand before unknown *men*." Joseph was put into the prison by Potiphar, but called from the prison by Pharaoh, a higher-ranking authority. What appeared to be a demotion was preparation for the promotion!

But without faith *it is* impossible to please *Him*, for he who comes to God must believe *that* He is, and that He is a rewarder of those who diligently seek Him.

Hebrews 11:6

To diligently seek, means to diligently *do*. Joseph practiced his gift of administration as a slave in Potiphar's house and as an inmate in the prison; doing all things as unto the Lord. Acting on this principle elevated Joseph from the bottom to the top in both settings. Joseph overcame each obstacle with the weapon of obedience. Jesus gave a description, in the Sermon on the Mount, of what diligently seeking Him looks like.

> Ask, and it will be given to you; seek, and you will find; knock, and it will be opened to you. For everyone who asks receives, and he who seeks finds, and to him who knocks it will be opened.
>
> Matthew 7:7-8

Asking takes place in prayer - inquiring of the Lord. Seeking is the doing of the strategic plan God revealed in the place of prayer. Knocking is the fulfillment of the strategic plan and announces, *I am in position to enter this door.*

The Bible doesn't give us a written account of Joseph's prayers along the way. He was fueled by faith in what God already showed him by the spirit as a seventeen-year-old boy. Years of seeking, doing all things as unto the Lord, and practicing his God-given gifts, are clearly documented. As he stood before Pharaoh, Joseph was in position to walk through this next door of elevation.

Enter the Open Door

Joseph had an opportunity to do what all the magicians of Egypt and all its wise men could not. Joseph was ready to put the power of God on display! As a seventeen-year-old boy, Joseph had two dreams that had not yet come to pass. Thank God for Joseph's time in the prison when and where he exercised his God-given gift of dream interpretation. Joseph interpreted the dreams of the baker and the butler, which both already transpired. This affirmed to Joseph the validity of his gift.

People are packaged with a spectrum of abilities and passions. Think of a brand-new puzzle. The picture on the box cover is like vision. *All* the pieces in the box join in some way, piece by piece, as a doer of the work strategically moves them. As Joseph interpreted the dreams of Pharaoh, God revealed through the mouth of Pharaoh the connection between Joseph's gifts.

This is the thing which I have spoken to Pharaoh. God has shown Pharaoh what He is about to do. Indeed seven years of great plenty will come throughout all the land of Egypt; but after them seven years of famine will arise, and all the plenty will be forgotten in the land of Egypt; and the famine will deplete the land. So the plenty will not be known in the land because of the famine following, for it *will be* very severe. And the dream was repeated to Pharaoh twice because the thing is established by God, and God will shortly bring it to pass. "Now therefore, let Pharaoh select a discerning and wise man, and set him over the land of Egypt. Let Pharaoh do *this*, and let him appoint officers over the land, to collect one-fifth *of the produce* of the land of Egypt in the seven plentiful years. And let them gather all the food of those good years that are coming, and store up grain under the authority of Pharaoh, and let them keep food in the cities. Then that food shall be as a reserve for the land for the seven years of famine which shall be in the land of Egypt, that the land may not perish during the famine." So the advice was good in the eyes of Pharaoh and in the eyes of all his servants. And Pharaoh said to his servants, "Can we find *such a one* as this, a man in whom is the Spirit of God?" Then Pharaoh said to Joseph, "Inasmuch as God has shown you all this, *there* is no one as discerning and wise as you. You shall be over my house, and all my people shall be ruled according to your word; only in regard to the throne will I be greater than you." And Pharaoh said to Joseph, "See, I have set you over all the land of Egypt."

Genesis 41:28-41

Pharaoh concluded that the one with the ability to interpret the dreams and announce the solution from God to preserve and prosper Egypt, is the same one who is more than qualified to administer the plan. Two of Joseph's gifts: the interpretation of dreams and administration bound together, solidifying Proverbs 18:16, "A man's gift makes room for him, And brings him before great men."

Due season sprang forth. Joseph was marked with Pharaoh's signet ring, garments of fine linen, and a gold chain; and rode in the second chariot while it was proclaimed, "Bow the knee!" In addition, Joseph was given Asenath as his wife (*see* Genesis 41:42-45) and she bore him two sons during the years of plenty.

Joseph named his sons: Manasseh, meaning, "for God has made me forget all my toil and all my father's house;" and Ephraim meaning, "for God has caused me to be fruitful in the land of my affliction" (*see* Genesis 41:51-52). Unbeknownst to Joseph, this was just the beginning of what Jehovah Gmolah, *the God of Recompense*, had in store for him!

OBEDIENCE OVERCOMES OBSTACLES

Idolatry

As Joseph was the assigned prophet to Pharoah at such a pertinent time, Daniel was to Nebuchadnezzar the king. Nebuchadnezzar was *so* troubled by the dreams he had, that his sleep left him. He began seeking a genuine interpretation of his dreams.

Like Pharoah, Nebuchadnezzar also sought help from the ungodly, who were unable to produce results. Nebuchadnezzar sought someone who could not only interpret his dreams but tell him the dreams. The magicians, astrologers, sorcerers, and the Chaldeans were perplexed and expressed the impossibility of being able to tell the king the dreams *he* had and to *then* interpret them (*see* Daniel 2).

Daniel entered Babylon as a captive. Daniel was one of God's elect, targeted by the enemy to be trained up in the Chaldean system of worldly pleasures and idolatry. Daniel remained faithful and true to His God and denied the momentary pleasures of the system that desired and actively worked to recruit him.

When Daniel found out about the urgent decree to put the wisemen to death for being unable to solve the king's problem, Daniel requested time to petition the Lord. The secret was then revealed to Daniel in a night vision.

Nebuchadnezzar was overwhelmed with gratefulness, but ultimately allowed pride to infiltrate him. The king took the vision God gave him of the large statue with the golden head and built for himself an all-gold statue and made a decree, *"that* at the time you hear the sound of the horn, flute, harp, lyre, *and* psaltery, in symphony with all kinds of music, you shall fall down and worship the gold image that King Nebuchadnezzar has set up; and whoever does not fall down and worship shall be cast immediately into the midst of a burning fiery furnace" (Daniel 3:5-6).

James 1:17 explicitly explains, "Every good gift and every perfect gift is from above, and comes down from the Father of lights, with whom there is no variation or shadow of turning." The initial interpretation of the dream validated Nebuchadnezzar's appointed position as ruler:

> ""This *is* the dream. Now we will tell the interpretation of it before the king. You, O king, *are* a king of kings. For the God of heaven has given you a kingdom, power, strength, and glory; and wherever the children of men dwell, or the beasts of the field and the birds of the heaven, He has given *them* into your hand, and has made you ruler over them all—you *are* this head of gold.["]
>
> Daniel 2:36-38

However, Nebuchadnezzar's pride and wicked-ness twisted the revelation he received from God (inter-preted through Daniel).

 **G**ain **S**trength Many Christians become discouraged when they are surrounded by unbelievers day after day at the workplace, in school, or even at home. We must have the realization and confidence that we have been sent as an oracle of God's light to bring revelation at the opportune time. Joseph nor Daniel had to solicit their opportunity or appointment. They were both sought out for the solution because of their reputation of faith, excellence, and understanding.

Obedience is a relevant principle of God
that produces extraordinary results over time!

Operating in obedience is about what you do in do season!
Do not grow weary because you will reap in due season! The
harvest of obedience always follows dew season!

And let us not grow weary while doing good,
for in due season we shall reap if we do not lose heart.
Galatians 6:9

Write unto the Lord

What reoccurring situation has brought you discouragement? As you remain committed to the process, how will you gain strength for your journey?

_____
_____
_____
_____
_____
_____
_____
_____
_____
_____
_____
_____
_____
_____
_____
_____
_____
_____
_____
_____
_____
_____
_____
_____
_____

Do, Due, Dew

Joseph faithfully executed the plan of God during the seven years of plenty. In Genesis 41:49 we are told, "Joseph gathered very much grain, as the sand of the sea, until he stopped counting, for it was immeasurable."

Mathematically, the plan to store one-fifth, or twenty percent, of the harvest during the seven years of plenty to sustain seven years of famine did not make sense. How could twenty percent of grain feed hundred percent of Egypt during seven years of famine?

The twenty percent that was sown into the storehouse became sustaining provision. The sacrifice of obedience yielded an overflowing return; proof that when followed, God's financial system triumphs the natural financial system. Even surrounding nations, who never sowed into the Egyptian storehouses, were sustained during the famine.

Joseph's father and brothers were in the land of Canaan experiencing the effects of the famine. In pursuit of relief, Jacob challenged ten of his sons to go to Egypt to buy grain that they may live and not die. In fear, Jacob refused to allow his youngest son Benjamin to make the journey.

Now Joseph was governor over the land; and it was he who sold to all the people of the land. And Joseph's brothers came and bowed down before him with *their* faces to the earth. Joseph saw his brothers and recognized them, but he acted as a stranger to them and spoke roughly to them. Then he said to them, "Where do you come from?" And they said, "From the land of Canaan to buy food." So Joseph recognized his brothers, but they did not recognize him. Then Joseph remembered the dreams which he had dreamed about them, and said to them, "You *are* spies! You have come to see the nakedness of the land!"

Genesis 42:6-9

This was the manifestation of Joseph's first dream noted in Genesis 37:7, "There we were, binding sheaves in the field. Then behold, my sheaf arose and also stood upright; and indeed your sheaves stood all around and bowed down to my sheaf."

As governor, assigned to administer the grain, Joseph interacted with multitudes of people – both Egyptians and people from other countries. Notice how Joseph recognized his brothers, but his brothers did not recognize him. The glory of God on Joseph's life brought visible change to his appearance, but his brothers remained the same.

Joseph spoke the language of the land of plenty and communicated with his brothers through an interpreter; while his brothers continued to speak the plaguing language of regret, fear, and lack.

Negotiations for Benjamin

Joseph accused his brothers of being spies. Joseph directed one of them to return home and present Benjamin in exchange for the life of the nine, who he intended to hold in Egypt.

So he put them all together in prison three days. Then Joseph said to them the third day, "Do this and live, *for* I fear God: If you *are* honest *men*, let one of your brothers be confined to your prison house; but you, go and carry grain for the famine of your houses. And bring your youngest brother to me; so your words will be verified, and you shall not die." And they did so. Then they said to one another, "We *are* truly guilty concerning our brother, for we saw the anguish of his soul when he pleaded with us, and we would not hear; therefore this distress has come upon us." And Reuben answered them, saying, "Did I not speak to you, saying, 'Do not sin against the boy'; and you would not listen? Therefore behold, his blood is now required of us." But they did not know that Joseph understood *them*, for he spoke to them through an interpreter. And he turned himself away from them and wept. Then he returned to them again, and talked with them. And he took Simeon from them and bound him before their eyes.

Genesis 42:17-24

After Joseph put his brothers in prison for three days, obedience to the principles of God overshadowed his emotions. His family in Canaan needed grain, so Joseph released nine of his brothers to carry the grain and kept Simeon as a negotiation tool for Benjamin.

In addition to filling his brothers' sacks with grain, Joseph gave a command for every man's money to be restored to him and for provisions to be given for the journey (*see* Genesis 42:25). Romans 12:21 emphasizes,

"Do not be overcome by evil, but overcome evil with good." Actively haunted by their actions from over twenty years ago, Joseph's brothers were terrorized by the blessing they were given.

> So he said to his brothers, "My money has been restored, and there it is, in my sack!" Then their hearts failed *them* and they were afraid, saying to one another, "What is this *that* God has done to us?"
>
> Genesis 42:28

> Then it happened as they emptied their sacks, that surprisingly each man's bundle of money *was* in his sack; and when they and their father saw the bundles of money, they were afraid.
>
> Genesis 42:35

Joseph's brothers told their father what took place in Egypt and the request for Benjamin. Operating from a place of brokenness and bitterness, Jacob was unwilling to trust God with Benjamin and chose to meditate on *if God doesn't come through* scenarios.

Jacob did not have the hindsight to know that when he released Benjamin, he would receive him back along with Simeon, Joseph, and the splendor of Goshen for his descendants. Lacking the confidence to release Benjamin prolonged the gift of recompense from being activated in his life.

> And Jacob their father said to them, "You have bereaved me: Joseph is no *more*, Simeon is no *more*, and you want to take Benjamin. All these things are

against me." Then Reuben spoke to his father, saying, "Kill my two sons if I do not bring him *back* to you; put him in my hands, and I will bring him back to you." But he said, "My son shall not go down with you, for his brother is dead, and he is left alone. If any calamity should befall him along the way in which you go, then you would bring down my gray hair with sorrow to the grave."

Genesis 42:36-38

Reuben was the one who influenced his brothers not to kill Joseph and to instead put Joseph in the pit where he planned to retrieve him from later. Reuben's delay to do what was right resulted in him missing that window of opportunity. Jacob was unaware of Reuben's past regret. However, with bold assurance, Reuben made a plea to his father to give him the chance to redeem himself, but Jacob refused.

When they had eaten up all the grain from the first trip to Egypt, Jacob beckoned for his sons to make a second trip. Judah, who originally initiated the idea to sell Joseph for profit, reminded Jacob that they would not be able to negotiate for grain without bringing Benjamin (*see* Genesis 43:1-9).

For if we had not lingered, surely by now we would have returned this second time." And their father Israel said to them, "If *it must be so*, then do this: Take some of the best fruits of the land in your vessels and carry down a present for the man—a little balm and a little honey, spices and myrrh, pistachio nuts and almonds. Take double money in your hand, and take back in your hand the money that was returned in the mouth of your sacks; perhaps it was an oversight. Take your brother also, and arise, go back to the man. And may God Almighty give you mercy before the man, that he may release your other brother and Benjamin. If I am bereaved, I am bereaved!"

Genesis 43:10-14

As the need for food became an urgent matter, and there was no possible way to meet the need otherwise, Israel yielded the results over to God. Jacob came to the end of himself *again*. Discern the way the names Jacob and Israel are being used in these verses. Emotional language is being credited to Jacob, while assertions made in faith are attributed to Israel.

In comparison, when Jacob prepared to reunite with his twin brother Esau, he sent presents ahead of him, seeking a peaceful encounter. Here again, presents and double money are prepared, desiring to appease the governor. These presents could be considered *bribes* to influence results; however, they were more so *offerings* exalting the importance of relationships over possessions.

Joseph's brothers arrived in Egypt for the second time, now with Benjamin, and were greeted by Joseph. Joseph commissioned the steward of his house to take his brothers to his home and prepare a feast.

Now the men were afraid because they were brought into Joseph's house; and they said, *"It is because of the money, which was returned in our sacks the first time, that we are brought in, so that he may make a case against us and seize us, to take us as slaves with our donkeys."*

Genesis 43:18

Anguished in their minds because of their past transgressions, Joseph's brothers were blind to the turning point of elevation and reconciliation about to take place in their lives.

At the door of Joseph's house, they explained to the steward that their money had been returned in their sacks after their first trip to buy food and they had brought it back along with additional money to buy food again. "But he said, 'Peace *be* with you, do not be afraid. Your God and the God of your father has given you treasure in your sacks; I had your money.' Then he brought Simeon out to them" (Genesis 43:23).

Joseph's brothers were received in his home with great hospitality. When Joseph entered, he was paid homage by his brothers. They bowed before him and presented their gifts. Joseph had not yet revealed himself to his brothers, and he inquired about their father who they reported was in good health and still alive.

Joseph saw his brother Benjamin. His heart yearned for him; being unable to compose himself, Joseph temporarily went into his chamber to weep. Customary seating was followed, putting Joseph, an

Egyptian, separate from his Hebrew brothers. It is also noted that Benjamin's serving of food was five times as much as his brothers (*see* Genesis 43:24-34).

The time of his brothers' departure drew near, and Joseph executed a plan to take Benjamin from among his brothers by making it appear as if he stole Joseph's cup. When Joseph's brothers were overtaken and inter-rogated by Joseph's steward, they were confident they were clear of any wrongdoing pertaining to *this* accu-sation. Their belongings were searched, and Joseph's cup was discovered in Benjamin's sack. They tore their clothes, removing even the thinnest layer of separation between themselves and God, signifying complete sur-render and a petition for mercy. They were returned to Joseph's house (*see* Genesis 44:1-15).

> Then Judah said, "What shall we say to my lord? What shall we speak? Or how shall we clear ourselves? God has found out the iniquity of your servants; here we are, my lord's slaves, both we and *he* also with whom the cup was found." But he said, "Far be it from me that I should do so; the man in whose hand the cup was found, he shall be my slave. And as for you, go up in peace to your father."
>
> Genesis 44:16-17

Judah kept his vow to his father and pleaded for Benjamin to be released. Judah told Joseph the words of Jacob, and Judah's vow to be a surety for the lad.

[A]nd the one [Joseph] went out from me, and I said, "Surely he is torn to pieces"; and I have not seen him since. But if you take this one [Benjamin] also from me, and calamity befalls him, you shall bring down my gray hair with sorrow to the grave.'
"Now therefore, when I [Judah] come to your servant my father, and the lad *is* not *with us*, since his life is bound up in the lad's life, it will happen, when he sees that the lad is not with us, that he will die. So your servants will bring down the gray hair of your servant our father with sorrow to the grave. For your servant became surety for the lad to my father, saying, 'If I do not bring him *back* to you, then I shall bear the blame before my father forever.'

Genesis 44:28-32

Judah demanded his life to be exchanged for the life of Benjamin. A change of heart was displayed by Judah. This activated an eruption within Joseph to reveal himself to his brothers.

Then Joseph said to his brothers, "I *am* Joseph; does my father still live?" But his brothers could not answer him, for they were dismayed in his presence. And Joseph said to his brothers, "Please come near to me." So they came near. Then he said: "I *am* Joseph your brother, whom you sold into Egypt. But now, do not therefore be grieved or angry with yourselves because you sold me here; for God sent me before you to preserve life. For these two years the famine *has been* in the land, and *there are* still five years in which *there will* be neither plowing nor harvesting. And God sent me before you to preserve a posterity for you in the earth, and to save your lives by a great deliverance. So now *it was* not you *who* sent me here, but God; and He has made me a father to Pharaoh, and lord of all his house, and a ruler throughout all the land of Egypt. "Hurry and go up to my father, and say to him, 'Thus says your son Joseph: "God has made me lord of all Egypt; come down to me, do not tarry. You shall dwell in the land of Goshen, and you shall be near to me, you and your children, your children's children, your flocks and your herds, and all that you have. There I will provide for you, lest you and your household, and all that you have, come to poverty; for *there are* still five years of famine."' "And behold, your eyes and the eyes of my brother Benjamin see that *it is* my mouth that speaks to you. So you shall tell my father of all my glory in Egypt, and of all that you have seen; and you shall hurry and bring my father down here." Then he fell on his brother Benjamin's neck and wept, and Benjamin wept on his neck. Moreover he kissed all his brothers and wept over them, and after that his brothers talked with him.

Genesis 45:3-15

Gain Strength

God is intentional. Our perspective is key in maintaining our momentum to endure times of testing. Joseph was fully convinced that he was walking in God's precepts for *his* life, "And God sent me before you to preserve a posterity for you in the earth, and to save your lives by a great deliverance. So now *it was* not you *who* sent me here, but God; and He has made me a father to Pharaoh, and lord of all his house, and a ruler throughout all the land of Egypt."

Isaiah 55:8-11
"For My thoughts *are* not your thoughts,
Nor *are* your ways My ways," says the Lord.
"For *as* the heavens are higher than the earth,
So are My ways higher than your ways,
And My thoughts than your thoughts.
"For as the rain comes down, and the snow from heaven,
And do not return there,
But water the earth,
And make it bring forth and bud,
That it may give seed to the sower
And bread to the eater,
So shall My word be that goes forth from My mouth;
It shall not return to Me void,
But it shall accomplish what I please,
And it shall prosper *in the thing* for which I sent it.

W**rite unto the** **L**ord

Reflect on some experiences and monumental points throughout your journey, where you are fully convinced it was only *His thoughts* and *His ways*, that brought forth results you were unable to even imagine at the time. What are some areas in your life now that you may feel are outside of your control, but you are determined to be diligent in knowing God has commissioned you to be *above only*?

Deuteronomy 28:13
And the Lord will make you the head and not the tail; you shall be above only, and not be beneath, if you heed the commandments of the Lord your God, which I command you today, and are careful to observe *them.*

Preparing for the Reunion

Joseph was seventeen years old the last time Jacob saw him. Twenty-two years had passed: Joseph was called before Pharaoh at the age of thirty; seven years of plenty were fulfilled; and Jacob was sent for after the second year of the famine.

> And Pharaoh said to Joseph, "Say to your brothers, 'Do this: Load your animals and depart; go to the land of Canaan. Bring your father and your households and come to me; I will give you the best of the land of Egypt, and you will eat the fat of the land. Now you are commanded—do this: Take carts out of the land of Egypt for your little ones and your wives; bring your father and come. Also do not be concerned about your goods, for the best of all the land of Egypt is yours.'" Then the sons of Israel did so; and Joseph gave them carts, according to the command of Pharaoh, and he gave them provisions for the journey.
>
> Genesis 45:17-21

With an abundance of provision for the journey, Joseph's brothers left Egypt and returned to the land of Canaan. Jacob was in disbelief when he heard the report, but the words of Jacob's sons were confirmed when he *saw* the carts which Joseph had sent to carry him.

> And they told him, saying, "Joseph *is* still alive, and he *is* governor over all the land of Egypt." And Jacob's heart stood still, because he did not believe

them. But when they told him all the words which Joseph had said to them, and when he saw the carts which Joseph had sent to carry him, the spirit of Jacob their father revived. Then Israel said, *"It is enough. Joseph my son is still alive. I will go and see him before I die."*

Genesis 45:26-28

Imagine Jacob's flood of emotions. He just heard that his beloved son Joseph, who he spent more years without than years with since his miraculous birth, was not dead but prospering.

Grief for Gladness

As a young boy, Joseph experienced loss and separation as did Jacob. Joseph lost his mother to death and his father to deception. How many times did Joseph probably fantasize about his father coming to rescue him from Egypt where he was held captive? Through it all, Joseph did not allow his present circumstances to paralyze him.

In Christ, life and death are temporary separations. Each person enters the earth through the womb of a woman for a short piece of time, to work as an ambassador. Then through the route of death, returns to infinite eternity. Jacob and Joseph had the opportunity to be reunited in the goodness of Goshen. Believers eagerly anticipate the heavenly reunion with the Lord Jesus Christ and their loved ones.

Jacob assumed that Joseph was dead based off of altered evidence; but the truth was that Joseph was alive, thriving, and within his reach! Deception hindered the truth from being clearly seen. Jacob spent decades bound to death even though he had breath in his body.

For Jacob to make the journey to Egypt he had to overcome confusion, fear, and complacency. He had to trust God again. Jacob's life was so tied to what he *thought* was Joseph's demise twenty-two years ago, that Jacob had become the walking dead.

Throughout Jacob's life he had open, reassuring communication with God from altar to altar. How did he become prey to this deception? As his own father Isaac did not seek after him; Jacob did not seek after Joseph. He blindly accepted defeat.

The thick, heavy, dark blanket of grief overtook Jacob and smothered him. It cut off his spiritual oxygen supply; which resulted in his spiritual fire dwindling. Fire needs oxygen, heat, and fuel to burn. Eliminating one component puts a fire out.

Before we come into a relationship with Jesus Christ, our state is the same. Jesus was sent as the great Light to expose the truth that darkness works to conceal. Jesus fulfilled the words that were spoken by Isaiah, the prophet, recorded in Matthew 4:16, "The people who sat in darkness have seen a great light, And upon those who sat in the region and shadow of death Light has dawned."

God breathed into Adam's nostrils the breath of life causing man to become a living being (*see* Genesis 2:7). With that same breath, we produce words. Proverbs

18:21 confirms, "Death and life *are* in the power of the tongue, And those who love it will eat its fruit."

The recorded words Jacob produced as he concluded Joseph was dead in Genesis 37:35 were, "For I shall go down into the grave to my son in mourning." And later in Genesis 42:36, "You have bereaved me: Joseph is no *more*, Simeon is no *more*, and you want to take Benjamin. All these things are against me." Jacob refused to be comforted and allowed his ears to be stopped up with grief and spoke in agreement with death. There is no indication in these chapters of Jacob speaking life, encouraging himself with the word, nor communicating with God at an altar.

In Genesis 45:27, we are told that, "the spirit of Jacob their father revived." Jacob returned to the sure way he knew to commune with God. As a young man, Jacob journeyed from his father's house in Beersheba toward Haran. He dreamed of a ladder and had an encounter with the Lord on the way. He established an altar that he called Bethel and exclaimed, "How awesome is this place! This is none other than the house of God, and this is the gate of heaven!" (Genesis 28:17).

On the reverse journey from Haran, Jacob eventually returned to Bethel. As discussed in Chapter 2, Jacob's name was changed and his charge was confirmed, "I *am* God Almighty. Be fruitful and multiply; a nation and a company of nations shall proceed from you, and kings shall come from your body" (Genesis 35:11).

Jacob later reunited with his father, Isaac, who was dwelling in Hebron, about twenty miles northeast of Beersheba. Jacob last saw Joseph in Genesis 37, when he sent Joseph to Shechem to check on his brothers. Hebron and Shechem are about fifty miles apart and Dothan, where Joseph was thrown into the pit, is about fifteen additional miles northwest from Shechem. There is no indication in the chapters discussed that Jacob returned to the *land* of his family: Beersheba, the land he originally set out from and God directed him back to in Genesis 31:13.

Now traveling southwest, en route to Egypt, Jacob passed through Beersheba and offered sacrifices to God. God spoke to him in visions of the night as recorded in Genesis 46:1-6. Pay attention to how the encounter opens. The Lord says, "Jacob, Jacob!" and Jacob responds, "Here I am."

We can conclude it has been at least fifty to sixty years since Jacob was in Beersheba. Jacob left Beersheba with no children and returned with his sons and his sons' sons; his daughters and his son's daughters; and all his descendants who came from his body, besides Jacob's sons' wives, were sixty-six persons in all (*see* Genesis 46:7 & 26). God fulfilled all He declared to Jacob in Genesis 28 when he went out:

> Now Jacob went out from Beersheba and went toward Haran. So he came to a certain place and stayed there all night, because the sun had set. And he took one of the stones of that place and put it at his head, and he lay down in that place to sleep.

Then he dreamed, and behold, a ladder *was* set up on the earth, and its top reached to heaven; and there the angels of God were ascending and descending on it. And behold, the LORD stood above it and said: "I *am* the LORD God of Abraham your father and the God of Isaac; the land on which you lie I will give to you and your descendants. Also your descendants shall be as the dust of the earth; you shall spread abroad to the west and the east, to the north and the south; and in you and in your seed all the families of the earth shall be blessed. Behold, I *am* with you and will keep you wherever you go, and will bring you back to this land; for I will not leave you until I have done what I have spoken to you."

Genesis 28:10-15

When Jacob returned to Beersheba, in Genesis 46, God released a word of assurance:

So Israel took his journey with all that he had, and came to Beersheba, and offered sacrifices to the God of his father Isaac. Then God spoke to Israel in the visions of the night, and said, "Jacob, Jacob!" And he said, "Here I am." So He said, "I *am* God, the God of your father; do not fear to go down to Egypt, for I will make of you a great nation there. I will go down with you to Egypt, and I will also surely bring you up *again*; and Joseph will put his hand on your eyes." Then Jacob arose from Beersheba; and the sons of Israel carried their father Jacob, their little ones, and their wives, in the carts which Pharaoh had sent to carry him. So they took their livestock and their goods, which they had acquired in the land of Canaan, and went to Egypt, Jacob and all his descendants with him.

Genesis 46:1-6

Despite what transpired along the way; God was faithful to do all He said He would do and more. Jacob fell short many times. Trouble came upon him and his family when he was out of position-caught in cycles of delay and emotional turmoil. But God...

For *there* is no sorcery against Jacob, Nor any divination against Israel. It now must be said of Jacob And of Israel, 'Oh, what God has done!'

Numbers 23:23

Henceforth, there is no sorcery against the old you (Jacob); nor any divination against the new you (Israel), that can void the vision God sent you into this earth to manifest. The witnesses; even the whispers, whiners, and wonderers, will be moved to declare, "Oh, what God has done!"

Perform the Word

On this earth we have one life to live. People are looking for answers. A Christian's response during tribulations testifies to the power of Christ. Triumphing in tragedy by standing firmly on the word of God and acting on His principles leaves a permanent impression with others. Performing the word makes the invisible visible.

By faith, we have the ability to *see* in the invisible realm and retrieve the blueprint for visible manifestation. The Lord said to Jeremiah, in Jeremiah 1:12, "You have seen well, for I am ready to perform My word." When the Angel announced to Mary that she was the chosen mother of Jesus, she grasped the seed needed for conception within her womb from the invisible realm. Her confession gave consent in Luke 1:38, "Behold the maidservant of the Lord! Let it be to me according to your word."

Gain Strength As it was *already* written with so many of the lives we have studied throughout this book, God has much more reserved for us than we are accessing. It is our own delay that is keeping us from *the* life of total fulfillment of God's precepts for us. The provision for every vision is on the way to the vision. To reinforce Deuteronomy chapter 9, as discussed in previous chapters, God continually challenges us to be in continuous expectation and pursuit of greater and mightier nations than ourself. It goes on to say, not because of our righteousness, but because of their wickedness. God is looking for yielded vessels of enforcement to activate 'on earth as it is in heaven' (*see* Matthew 6:10).

Deuteronomy 9:1, 5
"Hear, O Israel: You *are* to cross over the Jordan today, and
go in to dispossess nations greater and mightier than
yourself, cities great and fortified up to heaven,

It is not because of your righteousness or the uprightness
of your heart *that* you go in to possess their land,
but because of the wickedness of these nations *that* the Lord
your God drives them out from before you,
and that He may fulfill the word which the Lord
swore to your fathers, to Abraham, Isaac, and Jacob.

Write unto the Lord

Jesus told the Pharisees the kingdom of God does not come by observation, but the kingdom of God is within us. What is the specific word of God, for your life, that *must* be performed?

Develop What is *Right* for You

Luke 17:20-21
Now when He was asked by the Pharisees when the kingdom of God would come, He answered them and said, "The kingdom of God does not come with observation; nor will they say, 'See here!' or 'See there!' For indeed, the kingdom of God is within you."

You have also given me the shield of Your salvation; Your right hand has held me up, Your gentleness has made me great.

Psalm 18:35

11

Distinction

The Press Mold

Jacob was 130 years old when he embraced Joseph and they wept cleansing tears together in Goshen (*see* Genesis 47:9). Joseph could not be in Canaan and Egypt at the same time. Adversity pressed Joseph into the mold of his destiny. His pliability to be pressed allowed full manifestation of the mold. Under pressure, pliable clay takes on the defining features of the mold. Joseph's continued obedience to God's heart let him remain pliable through it all.

In contrast, transferring the articulate details of the mold is not possible using hardened clay. Israel was hardened and the pressure caused him to crumble. Grief sucked the living water necessary to live the abundant life out of Israel. This is evidenced in Genesis 46:30, "And Israel said to Joseph, 'Now let me die, since I have seen your face, because you *are* still alive.'"

God designed us for greater than *barely getting by* until the point of death. He wants to awaken the kingdom of God within us to experience His attributes on earth and in heaven. This is confirmed in the Lord's prayer recorded in Matthew 6:10, "Your kingdom come. Your will be done; On earth as it is in heaven." Choosing to escape the parameters of his past, Israel seized the chance to live heaven on earth in Goshen. He allowed the God of Recompense to saturate him with true life again.

Goodness of Goshen

Earth's provision ceased. The famine was severe throughout Egypt and surrounding nations. God opened the windows of heaven and released into Goshen an abundant reward as a direct result of Joseph's obedience.

The reward was more than grain to temporarily satisfy the stomach. Joseph's family was given the best of the land to dwell in, bread to eat, productive occupations, and dominion in a land of which they were strangers – elevating past its lifelong inhabitants.

> Then Pharaoh spoke to Joseph, saying, "Your father and your brothers have come to you. The land of Egypt *is* before you. Have your father and brothers dwell in the best of the land; let them dwell in the land of Goshen. And if you know *any* competent men among them, then make them chief herdsmen over my livestock." Then Joseph brought in his father Jacob and set him before Pharaoh; and Jacob blessed Pharaoh. Pharaoh said to Jacob, "How old *are* you?" And Jacob said to Pharaoh, "The days of the years of my pilgrimage *are* one hundred and thirty years; few and evil have been the days of the years of my life, and they

have not attained to the days of the years of the life
of my fathers in the days of their pilgrimage." So
Jacob blessed Pharaoh, and went out from before
Pharaoh.

Genesis 47:5-10

The Exchange

Now *there was* no bread in all the land; for the
famine *was* very severe, so that the land of Egypt
and the land of Canaan languished because of the
famine. And Joseph gathered up all the money that
was found in the land of Egypt and in the land of
Canaan, for the grain which they bought; and
Joseph brought the money into Pharaoh's house.
So when the money failed in the land of Egypt and
in the land of Canaan, all the Egyptians came to
Joseph and said, "Give us bread, for why should we
die in your presence? For the money has failed."
Then Joseph said, "Give your livestock, and I will
give you *bread* for your livestock, if the money is
gone." So they brought their livestock to Joseph,
and Joseph gave them bread in *exchange* for the
horses, the flocks, the cattle of the herds, and for
the donkeys. Thus he fed them with bread in
exchange for all their livestock that year. When
that year had ended, they came to him the next year
and said to him, "We will not hide from my lord
that our money is gone; my lord also has our herds
of livestock. There is nothing left in the sight of my
lord but our bodies and our lands. Why should we

die before your eyes, both we and our land? Buy us and our land for bread, and we and our land will be servants of Pharaoh; give *us* seed, that we may live and not die, that the land may not be desolate." Then Joseph bought all the land of Egypt for Pharaoh; for every man of the Egyptians sold his field, because the famine was severe upon them. So the land became Pharaoh's. And as for the people, he moved them into the cities, from *one* end of the borders of Egypt to the *other* end.

Genesis 47:13-21

Money was exchanged for grain until the money failed in both Egypt and Canaan. The Egyptians came to Joseph in lack. Joseph negotiated their livestock in exchange for the bread they craved.

Destructive decisions made in desperation caused the Egyptians to further entangle themselves in the bondage of poverty. The forfeited livestock was a source of power to work the fields; a mode of travel; and other animal resources, such as, meat, dairy, hides, horns, etc.

The famine had a set time to end but their *right now* urgency to appease the flesh superseded planning for the future.

With no means to produce or maintain provisions, the Egyptians next propositioned Joseph to buy their bodies and their lands in exchange for bread. They committed themselves and their land to be servants of Pharaoh, requested seed to work the land, and brought themselves under subjection of a taskmaster. Joseph moved the Egyptians into the cities and utilized the people to work the *very* land they just sold.

Tightening the Cord of Bondage

Notice the progression of language from verses 14-19 in Genesis 47. The first exchange was *money for grain*; then livestock; and later *their bodies and land for bread*. The final request was for seed to sow to benefit the one ruling over them.

Grain is reaped during harvest time. Bread is made from grain. Seed is sown to generate a crop. Remember, they experienced seven years of plenty and were carefreely consuming most of the harvest. Able to buy grain from the stocked storehouse, at the onset of the famine, they put their trust into money. Physical hunger sought relief, as lives were exchanged for bread. Confidence depleted as the cord of bondage tightened. A series of bad decisions drained their self-worth, and the Egyptians emotionally and physically yielded themselves to Pharaoh's system.

Given grain, one can choose how to prepare it for a meal. Feelings of helplessness shifted the request from grain to bread. Ready-made bread reduced the amount of effort on their part and, at the same time, eliminated choices. The expectation for productivity shifted from themselves to Pharaoh's governing system.

The Egyptians were transitioned from the vast broadness of their homes on large pieces of land to the confinements of their allotted, condensed living quarters in the cities. Now the property of Pharaoh, the

Egyptians were assigned to sow and work the same fields they once owned; with a mandate to give 20 percent to Pharaoh. Their portion of 80 percent was to be sown back into the land and used to feed their households (*see* Genesis 47:20-24).

Guess what? The seed sowed in the same ground they once owned by the *same* workers of the field, *themselves*, with the *same* abilities, yielded a harvest. The Egyptians were so excited to use their gifts and the resources they previously surrendered to glorify Pharaoh under bondage. In Genesis 47:25 they rejoiced, "You have saved our lives; let us find favor in the sight of my lord, and we will be Pharaoh's servants." This is perplexing. They prematurely cast away their confidence and subjected themselves to the vain repetition of the taskmaster, and were *excited*?

Gain Strength As employees, we agree to a predetermined income bracket and assigned hours of work when signing our employment contract. We are exchanging our time, talents, abilities, and obedience to standardized policies and procedures for a limited predetermined hourly wage or salary.

Most people consider using their time, talents, abilities, and obedience to the heavenly Voice alone, as too much risk, too much work, or too complex to navigate. Instead, settling for an employer to take the risk, assign the work, navigate *their* vision, and reap the uncapped benefits of their employees' labor (your labor), while the employee (you) reaps within the previously agreed upon income limits.

Remember Psalm 32:8 encourages us, "I will instruct you and teach you in the way you should go; I will guide you with My eye." Keep your eyes on Him, know His characteristics and expressions, yield to the course He navigated for you, and you will find perpetual strength for the journey.

Matthew 20:8-16

"So when evening had come, the owner of the vineyard said to his steward, 'Call the laborers and give them *their* wages, beginning with the last to the first.' And when those came who *were hired* about the eleventh hour, they each received a denarius. But when the first came, they supposed that they would receive more; and they likewise received each a denarius. And when they had received *it,* they complained against the landowner, saying, 'These last *men* have worked *only* one hour, and you made them equal to us who have borne the burden and the heat of the day.' But he answered one of them and said, 'Friend, I am doing you no wrong. Did you not agree with me for a denarius? Take *what is* yours and go your way. I wish to give to this last man *the same* as to you. Is it not lawful for me to do what I wish with my own things? Or is your eye evil because I am good?' So the last will be first, and the first last. For many are called, but few chosen."

Too often, the source of our frustration, is what *we agreed to*, despite our value being greater. We are working hard, from early in the morning, bearing the burden *and* the heat of the day, until late in the evening, and receiving less than what we desire.

The tile page of this book captures the thought, *"To be the chosen, you must come in agreement with the call. You are exempt from every disqualifier."* We must come in agreement with His call, as those referenced in Matthew 20:6-7 did. There was a group of people who did not start out at 6 am, 9 am, 12 pm, or 3 pm. They were still *standing idle in the marketplace* at the 11th hour (5 pm); "And about the eleventh hour he went out and found others standing idle, and said to them, 'Why have you been standing here idle all day?' They said to him, 'Because no one hired us.' He said to them, 'You also go into the vineyard, and whatever is right you will receive.'"

God is calling us, in this 11th Hour, from *standing idle* in the marketplace, into His vineyard, to utilize the gifts and talents we have perfected at a new level of distinction in the form of great exploits and entrepreneurship. It is time to *activate* the power that is within us to generate wealth, to establish His covenant, and to fulfill His promises to previous generations (*see* Deuteronomy 8:18). The only way to be able to direct profits, is to be *above only*. Unintentionally, we sow into things contrary to the word of God when retailers and investors direct the money we spend as consumers and generate as employees, into things we would not consciously support.

Standing indicates expectation. When an engine is *idle* it has all necessary parts and fuel to operate, *when* it is put into gear and the accelerator is engaged. Will you respond to the clarion call? We are not waiting for a *who*, it is His presence that activates the *present* in you!

Exodus 33:12-16

Then Moses said to the Lord, "See, You say to me, 'Bring up this people.' But You have not let me know whom You will send with me. Yet You have said, 'I know you by name, and you have also found grace in My sight.' Now therefore, I pray, if I have found grace in Your sight, show me now Your way, that I may know You and that I may find grace in Your sight. And consider that this nation *is* Your people." And He said, "My Presence will go *with you,* and I will give you rest." Then he said to Him, "If Your Presence does not go *with us,* do not bring us up from here. For how then will it be known that Your people and I have found grace in Your sight, except You go with us? So we shall be separate, Your people and I, from all the people who *are* upon the face of the earth."

Write unto the Lord

Reflect:

_____

_____

_____

_____

_____

CONFIDENCE

Therefore do not cast away your confidence, which has great reward. For you have need of endurance, so that after you have done the will of God, you may receive the promise: "For yet a little while, *And* He who is coming will come and will not tarry. Now the just shall live by faith; But if *anyone* draws back, My soul has no pleasure in him."

Hebrews 10:35-38

We cannot cast away our confidence; we need it to endure to the point of receiving the promise. The casting away of confidence is cunning and appears as:

- ❖ Believing God for everyone else's situation, except your own.
- ❖ Giving quality insightful advice to everyone else, except yourself.
- ❖ Performing with excellence at work, in church, and in the community; making everyone else look good, then returning home depleted and frustrated.

In fear, even the thought of failure brings condemnation and causes one to draw back. In confidence, there is no failure; only opportunity to perfect and spring forward. The *just* shall live by faith. The *just* are born-again believers, justified by the blood of Jesus Christ. Because of the blood, every spirit of destruction and untimely death working against the manifestation of the vision must pass over.

With vision, comes two types of provision. Provision to *do* the vision and provision generated *from* the completed work. God has so much He wants to get to us. Establishment of the vision creates an inlet so the immeasurable wealth of God can flow to us. When we reject carrying out the vision, we are rejecting God and His provision for us.

> Then the Lord said to Moses: "How long will these people reject Me? And how long will they not believe Me, with all the signs which I have performed among them?"
>
> Numbers 14:11

In Numbers 14, the majority of the people cast away their confidence, believing they were inadequate to possess the promise land that the Lord already declared, "I am giving to the children of Israel" in Numbers 13:2. Their perception of themselves as *grasshoppers* resulted in them forfeiting the very provision God already reserved for them (*see* Numbers 13:33).

Grasshoppers hop. Without confidence, a believer will hop in and out of places of destiny and allow vision to fade because of a lack of endurance; never receiving the promise. "For yet a little while, and He who is coming will come and will not tarry." Although, it may *seem* as if *it* is taking forever, continue. You are being perfected and strengthened to reap a mighty harvest. Once *it* comes, *it* will seem like it has always been there because it has; first in the invisible, now visible.

When we *draw back*, we reject the avenue God desires to use to make the invisible visible. The wind is invisible. What is visible, is the effect of the wind. Seeing something *move*, becomes evidence of the invisible wind. Move child of God; move! You are God's showpiece in the earth. Move in all He has for you; make the invisible visible! Refuse the snare of fear. Declaring the word of God brings us to the pinnacle of being fully persuaded! The *Lord is our confidence* and the word of God is the final authority in every situation!

> Do not be afraid of sudden terror, Nor of trouble from the wicked when it comes; For the LORD will be your confidence, And will keep your foot from being caught.
>
> Proverbs 3:25-26

> [T]o the intent that now the manifold wisdom of God might be made known by the church to the principalities and powers in the heavenly *places*, according to the eternal purpose which He accomplished in Christ Jesus our Lord, in whom we have boldness and access with confidence through faith in Him.
>
> Ephesians 3:10-12

> What then shall we say to these things? If God is for us, who *can be* against us?
>
> Romans 8:31

Dominion

Dominion is interwoven in every person. It is the desire to trump the current level. This is evident every time upgraded versions of products are created, crafted, and purchased: electronics, cars, clothes, foods, video games, etc.

Discern whose hands are forming your desire for dominion. A wicked potter will mold you to reign in an inferior realm. Made in the image and likeness of God, we have dominion over creation and everything that *creeps* (*see* Genesis 1:26). Obedience causes us to be *above only*, and never beneath (*see* Deuteronomy 28:13).

According to the Merriam-Webster Dictionary, the verb *creep* means to slip or gradually shift position; to move slowly to the ground. Paul cautions us in 2 Corinthians 11:3, "But I fear, lest somehow, as the serpent deceived Eve by his craftiness, so your minds may be corrupted from the simplicity that is in Christ." The serpent is a creep and caused a *creeping*, but in Christ, our covenant position is reinstated.

Beware of deception. The prefix de- means to *remove*; con- means *with*. Conception means to form or function. Deception is to remove, or abort, who God formed you to be and the function you were designed to carry out.

The *simplicity* that is in Christ is this: "For we are His workmanship, created in Christ Jesus for good works, which God prepared beforehand that we should walk in them" (Ephesians 2:10).

Surrounded by oppression, the priests were exempt from the regulations of the taskmaster, and the children of Israel prospered in Goshen (*see* Genesis 47:26-27). Jacob, an esteemed patriarch, basked in the splendor of his posterity for seventeen years in Goshen.

The Last Become First

Aware the time of Jacob's death was near; Joseph came to his father with his two sons. Jacob testified to the fulfillment of the words God had previously spoken to him (*see* Genesis 48:1-4). Ecstatic to see his grandsons, Israel said to Joseph in Genesis 48:11, "I had not thought to see your face; but in fact, God has also shown me your offspring!"

Joseph placed his sons Manasseh and Ephraim in position to be blessed by Jacob. Customarily, the first-born Manasseh was placed at Israel's *right* hand. Israel, however, maneuvered his hands to place his *right* hand on Ephraim. Jacob declared the blessing and accredited his grandsons to himself, as his own sons. Joseph assumed Jacob misplaced his hands and took his father's *right* hand to remove it from Ephraim's head to Manasseh's head:

And Joseph said to his father, "Not so, my father, for this *one is* the firstborn; put your right hand on his head." But his father refused and said, "I know, my son, I know. He also shall become a people, and he also shall be great; but truly his younger brother

shall be greater than he, and his descendants shall
become a multitude of nations."

Genesis 48:18-19

When Jacob crossed his arms and set the younger
Ephraim before the first-born Manasseh, he broke
tradition in response to the unction of the Spirit. While
Jacob was in the womb with his twin brother Esau, the
Lord spoke to their mother Rebekah and said, "the older
shall serve the younger" (Genesis 25:23). Esau, born first,
was the older, but Jacob received the blessing of the first
born.

Jesus explicitly taught about the *last becoming first*
and His detest for vain religious tradition. Being present
during *traditional* experiences such as church meals and
outreaches, but doing the works of iniquity, is enmity
with God (*see* Luke 13:23-26; James 4:4). Faltering
between two opinions, puts a person between enemy
lines on a battlefield: caught in the crossfire; but
unauthorized to access help because a true allegiance
was never formed with either side.

> But He will say, 'I tell you I do not know you, where
> you are from. Depart from Me, all you workers of
> iniquity.' There will be weeping and gnashing of
> teeth, when you see Abraham and Isaac and Jacob
> and all the prophets in the kingdom of God, and
> yourselves thrust out. They will come from the east
> and the west, from the north and the south, and sit
> down in the kingdom of God. And indeed there are

last who will be first, and there are first who will be last."

Luke 13:27-30

Right here in this text, is evidence of traditions being broken and the last becoming first. Jesus referenced imperfect men who became biblical pillars and multitudes of others, with a *willingness* to exchange their unrighteousness for His righteousness, *authorizing* entrance into the kingdom of God. To prophesize is to tell forth and reveal God's original intentions.

Romans 4:3 reminds us, "Abraham believed God, and it was accounted to him for righteousness." In previous chapters of this book, we looked at times in Abram's life when his faith was intimidated by his circumstances. As Abram exercised his faith, even when he was weak in faith; he grew to be able to produce the wonders of faith. Abraham's faith then intimidated and changed his circumstances. He is now referenced as our *father of faith* (*see* Romans 4:16).

Isaac, Jacob, and Joseph were birthed from barren women in a time when an unfruitful womb was viewed as a plague or a curse. Isaac was not the first born from his father's loins, but he was the *child of promise*.

Now we, brethren, as Isaac *was*, are children of promise. But, as he who was born according to the flesh [Ishmael] then persecuted him *who was born* according to the Spirit, even so it is now. Nevertheless what does the Scripture say? "Cast out the bondwoman and her son, for the son of the bondwoman shall not be heir with the son of the freewoman." So then, brethren, we are not children of the bondwoman but of the free.

Galatians 4:28-31

Persecution comes against things born according to the Spirit from things born according to the flesh. Power up in the Spirit and evict every circumstance, idea, emotion, and self-concept *born of the flesh* resulting in scoffing and agitation as Ishmael brought to Sarah (*see* Genesis 21:9-10). You are a child of promise; born into freedom. Untie – refuse to allow the weight of bondage to hinder your reign as heir. Elevate.

God qualifies the unqualified. Create this image in your mind: He plucked you *up and out* of the power of darkness; put you on the conveyor belt of His love to remove, restore, and replace; performing the work of redemption, producing *holiness* and *wholeness* spiritually, emotionally, and physically.

> [G]iving thanks to the Father who has qualified us to be partakers of the inheritance of the saints in the light. He has delivered us from the power of darkness and conveyed us into the kingdom of the Son of His love, in whom we have redemption through His blood, the forgiveness of sins.
>
> Colossians 1:12-14

> Jesus Christ *is* the same yesterday, today, and forever.
>
> Hebrews 13:8

Heaven and earth will pass away, but My words
will by no means pass away.

Matthew 24:35

The word of God is infallible and does not change.
Simultaneously, the Spirit of God moves in untraditional
ways. In Matthew 17:1-8, Jesus transfigured on a
mountain, and Moses and Elijah appeared alongside
Him. His disciples, Peter, James, and John were there.
Peter suggested they build three traditional tabernacles,
which was not the intent of the encounter. The voice of
God spoke from heaven and declared, "This is My
beloved Son, in whom I am well pleased. Hear Him!" (*see*
Matthew 17:5). God does not want to be boxed in by
religion that stifles communication with the One who
speaks from heaven. "For the word of God *is* living and
powerful, and sharper than any two-edged sword,
piercing even to the division of soul and spirit, and of
joints and marrow, and is a discerner of the thoughts and
intents of the heart" (Hebrews 4:12).

God gave precise, detailed instructions, throughout Exodus 26, of the dimensions, fine materials, colors,
designs, and precious metals to create the curtains used
in the tabernacle. Beautifully adorned and beholding
great value, these very curtains divided up the
tabernacle and restricted most people from being able to
enter the Most Holy Presence of God.

When Jesus was crucified, "the veil of the temple
was torn in two from top to bottom" (Mark 15:38). As a
result, the declaration in Hebrews 4:16 became our
reality, "Let us therefore come boldly to the throne of

grace, that we may obtain mercy and find grace to help in time of need." Traditions have a time and purpose, but do not supersede revelation. Revelation is the ability to hear, understand, and access the power to do the things God is speaking.

After blessing his grandsons, Jacob called for his sons. Further confirmation of Leah's covenant position in Jacob's life is evident in the order Jacob prophesied to his sons: Leah's six biological sons first, followed by the four sons of the maids, and lastly Rachel's two sons.

Here we will look at Jacob's last words to the sons we have discussed in this book.

Reuben, complimented, then ridiculed for being, "unstable as water, you shall not excel, because you went up to your father's bed; then you defiled *it*," (*see* Genesis 49:3-4); referencing when Reuben laid with Bilhah.

Simeon and Levi, "cursed *be* their anger, for *it* is fierce" (*see* Genesis 49:5-7); referencing when they slaughtered those who defiled their sister.

Judah, "highly esteemed and established according to his name of praise" (*see* Genesis 49:8-12). Judah displayed a contrite heart of repentance and was refreshed. King David and Jesus Christ arose from the tribe of Judah.

Joseph, his life was poetically stated. A *bough* is the main branch of a tree, thriving from the source of the well. Targeted by archers; but guarded by the blessing and excelling above limitation to elevation.

Joseph is a fruitful bough, A fruitful bough by a well; His branches run over the wall. The archers have bitterly grieved him, Shot at *him* and hated him. But his bow remained in strength, And the arms of his hands were made strong By the hands of the Mighty *God* of Jacob (From there is the Shepherd, the Stone of Israel), By the God of your father who will help you, And by the Almighty who will bless you *With* blessings of heaven above, Blessings of the deep that lies beneath, Blessings of the breasts and of the womb. The blessings of your father Have excelled the blessings of my ancestors, Up to the utmost bound of the everlasting hills. They shall be on the head of Joseph, And on the crown of the head of him who was separate from his brothers.

Genesis 49:22-26

Benjamin, "is a ravenous wolf; In the morning he shall devour the prey, And at night he shall divide the spoil" (Genesis 49:27). What was spoken reflected both the name Ben-Oni, son of my sorrow given by his mother; and Benjamin, son of my right hand given by his father. A ravenous wolf is more concerned *that* it is consuming than with *what* it is consuming. Rachel was consumed by death at Benjamin's birth and Jacob's time with Simeon and Joseph was consumed when Jacob initially refused to release him. King Saul, who reigned before David in the Old Testament, and Saul, who became Paul in the New Testament, are accredited to the tribe of Benjamin (*see* 1 Samuel 9:21 and Romans 11:1). *Ravenous wolves*: both destroyed yet produced.

Jacob's Death

Symbolically, seventy days of mourning took place after the death of Jacob. Possibly, a day for each life that escaped the shadow of death cast during the famine, guided into the light of Goshen. A prestigious procession accompanied Joseph from Egypt to Jacob's chosen final resting place, where his wife, Leah, parents, and grandparents were buried.

> So Joseph went up to bury his father; and with him went up all the servants of Pharaoh, the elders of his house, and all the elders of the land of Egypt, as well as all the house of Joseph, his brothers, and his father's house. Only their little ones, their flocks, and their herds they left in the land of Goshen. And there went up with him both chariots and horsemen, and it was a very great gathering.
>
> Genesis 50:7-9

Residue

Sticky residue from evil plots accumulated layers of dark dust distorting and veiling the view of reconciliation. Joseph's brothers believed it had been the life of their father who withheld their deserved wrath looming from their youth.

> When Joseph's brothers saw that their father was dead, they said, "Perhaps Joseph will hate us, and may actually repay us for all the evil which we did to him." So they sent *messengers* to Joseph, saying, "Before your father died he commanded, saying,

'Thus you shall say to Joseph: "I beg you, please forgive the trespass of your brothers and their sin; for they did evil to you."' Now, please, forgive the trespass of the servants of the God of your father." And Joseph wept when they spoke to him. Then his brothers also went and fell down before his face, and they said, "Behold, we *are* your servants." Joseph said to them, "Do not be afraid, for *am* I in the place of God? But as for you, you meant evil against me; *but* God meant it for good, in order to bring it about as *it is* this day, to save many people alive. Now therefore, do not be afraid; I will provide for you and your little ones." And he comforted them and spoke kindly to them.

Genesis 50:15-21

Joseph's second dream was fulfilled. "The sun, the moon, and the eleven stars bowed down" to a greater degree than projected by his father: "Shall your mother and I and your brothers indeed come to bow down to the earth before you?" (Genesis 37:9-10).

The inhabitants of the foreign land of Egypt were commanded to *bow the knee* (*see* Genesis 41: 43). When his brothers came to Egypt to first buy grain they, "bowed down before him with *their* faces to the earth" (*see* Genesis 42:6). During his brothers second trip to Egypt they, "bowed down before him to the earth," and, "bowed their heads down and prostrated themselves" (*see* Genesis 43:26 & 28).

Customarily and halfheartedly people bow to positions. This does not equate to wholehearted honor or surrender to the authority. Now, thirty-nine years after their transgression (twenty-two years of separation and seventeen years together in Goshen), Joseph's brothers finally released themselves from the inner enemy of self-unforgiveness. This is evident as they fell down before his face, and they said, "Behold, we are your servants" (*see* Genesis 50:18).

When a person traditionally *bows*, they are in control of their movements. As they *fell down*, they relinquished all physical, mental, and emotional control. Until the moment they *fell down*, they were still trying to reason and finagle the circumstances. There is nowhere in the text that confirms their father petitioned for Joseph to forgive his brothers. Neither is it noted if Jacob ever found out the truth about how Joseph ended up in Egypt.

For the first thirty years of his life, Joseph was in a cycle of sudden highs and sudden lows. Joseph was loved by his father but hated by his brothers; lavished in the robe of many colors and given prophetic dreams, yet isolated. He grew to be highly esteemed in Potiphar's house, but treated as property by Potiphar's wife. Joseph was sentenced to prison without a chance to state his case. He became authoritative in the prison but remained subject to the parameters of confinement. Hope arose that the butler would testify on his behalf, but it was two more years until Joseph was mentioned and that cycle was broken.

Joseph lived 110 years. Thirty years of sowing followed by eighty years of reaping. Here are Joseph's final prophetic words that came to pass over time:

> And Joseph said to his brethren, "I am dying; but God will surely visit you, and bring you out of this land to the land of which He swore to Abraham, to Isaac, and to Jacob." Then Joseph took an oath from the children of Israel, saying, "God will surely visit you, and you shall carry up my bones from here."
>
> Genesis 50:24-25

Obedience overcomes obstacles. Joseph is a firsthand account of the benefits of submission to God. Elevation is guaranteed when we align ourselves under His mission. Walking under the covering of the Divine umbrella diverts the outpouring of resistance past the one in alignment, causing it to fall under foot. Obedience puts us in position to trample adverse circumstances, dispossess greater and mightier nations than ourselves, and establish dominion over every place the soles of our feet tread.

> For if you carefully keep all these commandments which I command you to do—to love the LORD your God, to walk in all His ways, and to hold fast to Him— then the LORD will drive out all these nations from before you, and you will dispossess greater and mightier nations than yourselves. Every place on which the sole of your foot treads shall be yours... Deuteronomy 11:22-24

Lightning Source UK Ltd.
Milton Keynes UK
UKHW010136030821
388208UK00001B/148